INSIDE THE BANK OF ENGLAND

INSIDE
The Bank of England

Philip Geddes

Contents

To Selina with much love

Acknowledgements

This book arose out of a documentary made about the Bank by Television South, a programme of which I was the producer and director. I should like to thank Peter Williams, Controller of Factual Programmes, for asking me to make the programme; also for his encouragement of the book. I am also most grateful for the enormous help given by Dominic Scott, the researcher on the film, and Peter Hobday, who presented it.

My greatest debt is to all those at the Bank of England who gave so freely of their time and expertise to explain the workings of the Bank. In particular I must thank Philip Warland, Head of the Information Division, and his colleagues in the Division, especially Roger Mayes and Paul Wright, for their patience and generous assistance. I must also thank John Keyworth, Archivist of the Bank, for his much-valued comments on the historical sections of the book, and Terry Bell and his colleagues in the Bank's Reference Library. In addition I am grateful to all those in the Bank who talked to me about their specialist areas: especially the Deputy Governor George Blunden, Eddie George, David Walker, David Somerset, Brian Quinn, Ian Hill, Tony Coleby, Ian Thompson, Malcolm Gill, Bert Sharples, Roger Withington, Roger Lomax and Derek Byatt.

I am grateful to those in the City and at Westminster who gave help: particularly David Scholey, Lord Bruce-Gardyne, Denis Healey and Lord Donaghue. I must also thank all those elsewhere who provided me with material: including Guy Head, Michael Cobham, Elizabeth Gibson, Virginia Robertson, and my father,

David Geddes. For the photographs I am indebted to Tony Nutley and Bert Hill and the Bank. Thanks are also due to Sarah Mahaffy for her enthusiasm and support; and finally to my wife Selina, who has given me immense encouragement. I hope she feels this book is worth all those long months of patience.

P. G.

Photograph credits: 1a, 2, 3, 4 are reproduced by courtesy of the Governor and Company of the Bank of England. All other photographs are the copyright of Television South, with the exception of photograph 1, reproduced by courtesy of the BBC Hulton Picture Library.

List of Illustrations

1. James Gilray's cartoon 'Political Ravishment, or The Old Lady of Threadneedle Street in danger!' published in 1797.

1a. Montagu Norman, the Bank's longest-serving Governor, who served from 1920 to 1944.

2. Top left: one of the earliest surviving Bank of England notes, dated 1699.

3. Top right: a country-bank note, issued in 1825 by the Andover Bank.

4. Left: one of the last of the Bank of England's famous white fivers.

5. In this box are the Bank's 'giants' – million-pound notes never issued to the public, but which back the Scottish and Irish banks' note issue.

6. Bank printing works. Old notes which cannot be reissued are burned: this is £6 million worth of £5 notes going up in smoke.

7. Bank printing works. Newly printed notes being checked.

8. Bank printing works. Notes being sorted before reissue to eliminate 'foreign' ones , that is, Scottish notes.

9. Bank printing works. Roger Withington, artist-designer, working on detail of the design of the £50 note.

10. A face to match a well-known signature: Chief Cashier to the Bank, David Somerset, seated under a portrait of one of his most famous predecessors, Abraham Newland.

Introduction

'Nothing would persuade the English people to abolish the Bank of England; and if some calamity swept it away, generations must elapse before at all the same trust would be placed in any other equivalent.' That was the verdict of the Victorian political economist Walter Bagehot in *Lombard Street*, his famous book on banking published in 1873.

When Bagehot wrote his book, the Bank had been in existence for almost two centuries, and had become the pillar of the British financial system. As he put it, 'on the wisdom of the directors of that one joint stock company, it depends whether England shall be solvent or insolvent'. Today, more than a century later, the Bank is no longer a privately owned joint-stock company, but a publicly owned arm of government. Its influence is, if anything, greater and more pervasive than it was a century ago.

Yet the Bank is one of the least-known institutions in Britain and, until recently, took great pains to remain so. The attitude was well summed up by a member of the Bank's inner cabinet, the Committee of Treasury, who wrote to the Governor of the Bank in 1894 that is was 'wholly beneath the dignity of the Court that any of its members should be influenced by the ignorant comments of the Press. It would scarcely be more indecorous if they themselves were to influence such comments.' It was not until 1941 that the Bank appointed, with extreme reluctance, an 'Adviser' on dealing with the Press. (The present Governor is, in fact, the first to give on-the-record interviews to the media.) One of his predecessors, the great Montagu Norman, loathed the Press, and took immense pains to

1

avoid journalists, even to the extent of making all his travel bookings in the name of his personal secretary, Skinner. His view of the Bank's operations, as he put it to his colleagues, was 'never explain, never excuse'.

One powerful factor explains the Bank's reticence: many of its operations are market-sensitive, and a word in the wrong place could have major consequences. But there is another, less obvious reason: for many years it has been accustomed to being master in its own house; doing what it felt was needed in the economic life of the nation untrammelled by legal limitations or statutory restrictions. It has always preferred to operate in a quiet and informal way, and such methods of working require freedom from the spotlight of public interest. For many years the Bank has fought off assaults on its operational and practical independence – some from the Treasury, its nominal master, but mainly from Parliament, which has struggled in vain to make this least-public of publicly owned institutions more accountable to its proprietors.

And, while almost every other institution in British life – even, to some extent, the monarchy – has opened itself to the all-pervasive eye of the television camera over the last few years, the Bank has resisted such intrusions. But now the mood inside the Bank has changed. In the autumn of 1986, after lengthy negotiations, the Bank invited a film crew from Television South to make a film inside the Bank on its work. An extraordinary degree of access was given, and Bank officials opened the doors on the whole range of the Bank's activities.

For most people, the Bank is just the place where they make banknotes and intervene to protect sterling against speculation. Although these are two of the Bank's most publicly visible jobs, the range of its work is much wider. At the heart of its job is the management of the money and foreign-exchange markets. This involves influencing interest rates and the foreign-exchange rate. In addition the Bank is the legally appointed guardian of the banking system: it supervises and licenses anyone wishing to set up in business as a bank in the United Kingdom. The Bank is also a key part of the process of economic policy formulation in Britain; it advises the Treasury on economic matters and executes key aspects of policy. This arises out of one of its traditional functions, as banker to the Government. It keeps the Government's bank accounts and manages both the funding and the administration of the national debt. And there are other jobs the Bank undertakes, none of which has anything to do with its statutory duties or its role as the Government's banker: it exercises informal supervision over the City of London and the financial sector as a whole, and does not hesitate to intervene in the affairs of the City when it feels that intervention is required. On top of that, it has also taken on a role in managing the rescue of ailing industrial companies.

Perhaps its most important job in recent years, and one which may be the reason for the new policy of much more openness, is the part the Bank has played in the process of Big Bang: the deregulation of the City's financial markets which has opened them to world competition. It may well be that the Bank wishes its role to be seen and evaluated in public. It was the Bank that pushed the Stock Exchange into accepting that deregulation was necessary; it is the Bank that has quietly orchestrated the upheavals in the structure of the City that have followed. In so doing the Bank has taken an enormous risk: it has made a heavy investment of its prestige and authority in the hope that Big Bang will be good for Britain. If the City fails to meet that challenge the Bank will carry the blame for encouraging it in the first place.

These risks have been faced with the same sort of equanimity with which the Bank does all its work; for the overwhelming impression the outsider gets of the Bank is its air of irritatingly effortless superiority. Though Bank people do work hard, they still manage to give one the feeling that it is really quite an easy job. As Bagehot put it in *Lombard Street*, 'banking never ought to be an exceedingly laborious task'.

1

'An Elderly Lady of Great Credit and Long Standing'

At eleven o'clock each weekday morning, a dozen soberly dressed middle-aged men file into the magnificent office of the Governor of the Bank of England in Threadneedle Street. They are the senior management of the Bank, the heads of its various operating divisions. They sit on three sides of a square around the Governor's massive desk, heaps of documents and papers piled precariously on their knees. A ritual of central banking is about to begin – 'Books'. It is called 'Books' because it was originally the occasion at which the books of the Bank were presented to the Governor for inspection. Today 'Books' is the Bank's daily management information meeting. No one would think of changing the name of this ritual: it seems an inseparable part of the mystique of the Bank.

It is, as it were, the daily act of worship of a curious form of tribal religion that seems to have no connection with the sordid business of money-making. On the decisions made by these men will rest the fate of businesses, to say nothing of the price of mortgages. What they say and do will influence the enormous worldwide money machine outside the Bank, a massive industry employing hundreds of thousands of people. Central bankers such as those at 'Books' are at the heart of that industry in every country, watching and regulating, managing markets and currencies. Like spiders at the centre of the web, they weave the strong but almost invisible threads that keep the financial world going.

The ritual that surrounds the Bank of England is a reflection of its long and distinguished history as the instigator of that role round the world. As the grand old lady of central bankers, the Bank invented many of the techniques of control of the financial sector that are now used throughout the world.

The very age and dignity of the Bank seem to set it apart from the other banks, making it appear a very special institution. In a way this is true; but it is also an illusion carefully cultivated over the years. For, though the Bank of today is a very different animal from the commercial banks, it had its origins in the same market-place. To understand how the Bank of England came to its present position one must explain something of the process by which banking evolved.

For many years the world got along without bankers and there-fore without central bankers. Early banking grew out of the activities of merchants and traders. Through their normal business operations they tended to accumulate capital, surplus money which they wished to put to use. It was almost inevitable that kings and princes should be among their first clients. Unlike merchants. they tended to be spenders rather than accumulators of capital. Governments also, then as now, had the habit of spending more than they earned. This created deficits and thus a need for bankers to fund them.

In the Middle Ages, the Jews acted as bankers to the princes of Europe. The medieval laws of usury, with their strictures against the charging of interest, kept many Christians out of the lending business; but the Jewish community did not feel itself bound by these Christian laws. Kings connived at this; they needed the money, and knew that it could not be obtained without payment. It was therefore convenient for them to offer the Jews protection from the law. This put the Jewish moneylenders in a close and complex relationship with kings: reviled as usurers, they were none the less milked by successive monarchs as the only source of ready cash. But the relationship was never comfortable; neither side trusted the other, and there were frequent disputes between banker and customer. Eventually banker and client fell out and the Jews were expelled from a succession of European countries – they were ordered to leave England in 1290.

The departure of the Jews left a gap in the finances of many royal houses. This was filled by the first multinational bankers, the Lombards. They had spread across Europe from the plains of northern Italy, following the development of trade. Soon they found a profitable niche in meeting governments' needs for money. But, like the Jews before them, they too fell foul of the authorities. Just as modern bankers have, on occasion, found themselves in trouble lending to sovereign governments, so the Lombards discovered that it does not always pay to put your trust in princes. When Edward III repudiated his debt of 900,000 gold florins to the Bardi family and of 600,000 florins to the Peruzzis, both great banking houses collapsed.

The Lombards have, however, left us with a legacy: the coin they introduced into England – the florin – stayed with us, in name at least, until recent years; and the street in which they settled in London, Lombard Street, today retains both its name and its connection with banking.

The problem for both the Jews and the Lombards, and, for that matter, the kings with whom they dealt, was that neither side had much security. From the bankers' point of view, what was needed was some guarantee that a debt, once entered into, would be honoured. From the monarch's point of view, a guaranteed supply of money at a reasonable price was essential for survival.

The obvious solution – the creation of a permanent institution to channel money from merchants to government and manage the terms of such lending – was perceived by many, in England as well as elsewhere. In the century before the foundation of the Bank of England and even earlier, there appeared numerous pamphlets and proposals suggesting just such an institution. In 1581, for example, one Christopher Hagenbuck proposed to Queen Elizabeth that she establish a national bank. 'It shall keep the country in abundance and remove the extreme usuries that devour your Majesty and your people.'

Soon there was an example overseas to prove the point. England's greatest commercial rival, Holland, decided that as a trading nation it needed a central bank of exchange. The Bank of Amsterdam was therefore set up in 1609. It was essentially a traders' bank – dealing in foreign exchange and bill settlement rather than government debt – but its stability and prestige soon made it an example for those in England who wanted a bank for the nation's affairs. Other banks along similar lines were soon established in trading centres on mainland Europe.

In England the case for a national bank was made much stronger by the profligate habits of the Stuart kings. Both Charles I and Charles II faced the problems familiar to today's developing nations: a low level of economic development and therefore a narrow tax base, inadequate systems of revenue collection, and high inflation. Added to this was a fondness for the grandiose – a characteristic of many modern developing nations. All these factors ensured that both kings were perpetually short of cash. Charles I's problems with his parliament – in particular the touchy subject of the levying and spending of money – eventually led to the Civil War and his execution. It is worth going into one of the ways in which he tried to solve the problem, for in this instance the downright criminality of his actions much advanced the case for a national bank, and made him by default, as it were, the father of the Bank of England.

Since the downfall of the Lombards, London traders had taken to storing their excess money at the Crown Mint, then situated in the Tower of London, on the grounds that their money would be safe in the place where the King kept his. In 1640 Charles helped himself to £130,000 of merchants' money held in the Tower. The ensuing outcry at this act of robbery persuaded the King to return most of the money. At the same time his actions convinced the merchants that the monarch was not to be trusted, and that a better way to meet the Government's need for cash must be found – to say nothing of a safer place in which to store their money.

During the Civil War and the Protectorate proposals to create a national bank receded while the conflict between the authority of King and Parliament was settled. But the financial problems of government returned with the restoration of the monarchy in 1660. If anything they were worse, as one essential principle effectively conceded by the Crown during the Civil War was parliamentary control over the finances of the state.

Charles II solved his problems by borrowing from the only group who would lend to him, the goldsmiths. As their name implies, they were originally craftsmen in gold, but they had been turned into bankers almost by force of circumstance. As part of their trade, they had secure premises: merchants were willing to store their gold there. And, since the goldsmiths had spare money in their vaults, they lent it out. Despite the fact that the security for their loans to the Government was the income from future taxes, the poor level

8

of their confidence in the King was reflected in high rates of interest. At the beginning of his reign, Charles II found himself being charged 8 per cent for money – a steep figure for the time, but one that increased as his financial problems mounted. The diarist Samuel Pepys complained that the Treasury were 'forced to pay 15 or sometimes 20 per cent for their money, which is a most horrid shame, and that which must not be suffered'.

Despite this hardly generous help from the goldsmiths, Charles was still unable to match income to expenditure. Parliament, for its part, was reluctant to grant him the money to close the gap. This led to a financial crisis in 1672. The King had debts of £1.3 million and no income with which to pay them. Put in modern terms, his solution was default. On 2 January an Order in Council suspended all payments out of the Exchequer for twelve months. This ruined many merchants who had lent money to the Government from their deposits with the goldsmiths. Little of this money was ever repaid (although Charles, worried at the damage default would do to his credit rating, did at least attempt to settle with his creditors).

The revolution of 1688, and the accession to the throne of William and Mary, exacerbated the situation. England was now embroiled in the conflict between Holland and France, which led to a level of public expenditure far greater than Parliament was willing to sanction. William's financial situation on his accession was bleak: the total income available to him was a little more than £1.6 million. Of this just over £1 million had to meet the cost of an already inadequate army and navy. In time of war such forces – and such revenue – would clearly be inadequate.

William showed himself quite as ingenious as his Stuart predecessors in trying to fill the gap. A variety of clever taxes were devised. One, a stamp tax, is still with us. Others did not survive; they included a window tax, a pedlar tax, a coach tax, birth, death and marriage taxes, and – to catch all those who hadn't been caught by any of these levies – a bachelor tax. This taxed those who remained single – the cost of which was set at £12 11s. per annum for a duke. Less significant persons paid just a shilling a head. William also experimented with the rather more modern notion of a state lottery. It was intended that this should raise £2 million, with prizes of £40,000. In the event it drew in only £1 million.

Despite all these tactics, the Government still did not have enough money to wage war in Europe. It was a good time to reconsider the idea of a national bank. Numerous proposals for one had been produced, but the one taken up by the Government was that put forward by a young Scot from Dumfriesshire called William Paterson. Paterson had led an adventurous career around Europe, though he was still only in his thirties.

He now lived in London and was involved in politics and business. His proposal to the Treasury was that £1.2 million be raised from City merchants and lent to the Government in return for a yearly payment of £100,000 – in interest and management fees – and certain privileges. He suggested that the sum be raised by public subscription and that the subscribers become a corporation to manage this debt. The name he proposed was 'the Governor and Company of the Bank of England'. Paterson hoped that the creation of this institution would give security to the lenders of money, as well as supplying financial resources to the Government at a price it could afford. Inherent in this was the idea of permanent lending to the Government: today's National Debt.

The reasonableness of the notion was not universally apparent. The goldsmiths saw it as an attack on a very profitable line of business in which, until then, they had held a monopoly. Others outside the City were also hostile. The still-numerous supporters of the deposed James II saw it as a means of propping up the hated usurper William. The Tory country gentlemen, always suspicious of City money men, viewed it as a means of squandering yet more of England's gold on unending and useless foreign wars. Many in Parliament were unhappy too. Having just fought a civil war on the principle of parliamentary control of the executive's finances, the proposal looked suspiciously like a device to help the King by-pass Parliament.

Given such weight of opposition it is surprising that the Act establishing the Bank of England was passed at all. But in April 1694, after heated debate, it was. To assuage critics a clause was inserted prohibiting the Bank from lending money to the Government without the consent of Parliament. The Act itself does not actually mention the Bank at all in its title: formally it is 'An Act for granting to their Majesties several rates and duties upon tunnages of ships and vessels, and upon beer, ale and other liquors; for securing certain recompenses and advantages, in the said act mentioned, to such persons as shall voluntarily advance the sum of fifteen hundred thousand pounds towards carrying on the war against France.' The explanation for this curious title is that payment of the interest on the loan was secured against duties on shipping and alcohol. The Bank was in fact known to many in its early years as the 'Tunnage Bank'.

Few at the time saw the significance of what Parliament had done. To contemporaries it was just another ruse to raise money. The diarist John Evelyn noted on 24 April 1694, 'A publick bank of £140,000 [sic] set up by Act of Parliament among other Acts and Lotteries, for money to carry on the war – the whole month of April without rain'.

It says something for the reputation of the promoters, most of them well-known City names, that the full sum was raised from subscribers in a matter of a few days. The next item on the agenda was the election of a Governor, Deputy Governor and Court of Directors. As Governor the subscribers chose Sir John Houblon, a wealthy City merchant of Huguenot origin. His deputy was another well-respected figure, Michael Godfrey. By the end of July 1694 the new bank was in business.

The first sums towards the war efforts were handed over to the Government at the beginning of August, and by the end of the year all the funds originally promised had been delivered. In return the King met his side of the bargain. As promised, the Bank was granted certain privileges. It was allowed to issue notes, and deal in bills of exchange and bullion. The original charter granting these privileges was to run for twelve years.

But the Bank's position was still far from unchallenged. A rival proposal for a bank based not on gold and silver, but on land, was also given a warm reception by the Government. The principle was that land should be the asset against which a bank might lend money: a sort of early building society. This was a fine-enough concept provided land retained its value and its convertibility as gold did. The scheme naturally appealed to the country gentleman, who saw thereby a means of turning his main fixed asset into cash while retaining use of the asset itself. A bill establishing the Land Bank passed through Parliament with little opposition and the Bank of England braced itself for competition. Exultant supporters of the project even published an obituary of the Bank in newspapers.

11

The merchants of the City and other potential subscribers were not so easily fooled. At the end of three weeks the paltry sum of £2100 was all that had been raised. With so poor a response the Land Bank collapsed. To make up for the grand promises made by its promoters, the Bank of England raised a further £340,000 in loans to the Government so that the 1696 military campaign could start.

The failure of the Land Bank, though welcome, did not remove all the Bank of England's problems. The reminting of the aged and, in many cases, mutilated coinage of the realm caused a panic which led to a run on the Bank by nervous depositors. Only swift and effective action by the Governor, and enthusiastic support from many City merchants, prevented the new corporation from going the same way as the Land Bank.

Within a short time the new institution was sufficiently well established for its original proposer, William Paterson, to claim that 'the creation of this famous bank not only relieved the ministerial managers from their frequent processions into the City for borrowing money ... at 10 or 12 per cent per annum, but likewise gave life and currency to double or treble the value of its capital in other branches of the public credit, and so under God, became the principal means of the success of the campaign in 1695'.

The death of Queen Anne in 1714 and the subsequent Jacobite Rebellion of 1715 presented a threat to the Bank's growing stability. The Bank was, after all, one of the main beneficiaries – and supporters – of the 1688 Revolution that had brought William and Mary to the throne. The Jacobite aim of placing the Pretender on the throne and ending conflict with France was hardly in the interests of those who were profiting from that conflict. The years of war had been good for the Bank, with each new campaign leading to a further call for funds, for which the Government paid handsomely in the form of interest. In return for meeting these calls promptly, the Bank had also been able to exact useful privileges that had considerably strengthened its position as a private company. In return for a loan granted in 1697, for example, the Government had agreed that no rival bank should be established by charter; and property of the Bank was declared exempt from tax.

The Jacobite Rebellion was not in itself damaging, although it caused a temporary run on the Bank. The end of the war in Europe, on the other hand, produced a different sort of threat. The Bank found itself embroiled in a situation in which its financial strength was severely tested – a crisis which moved it towards a role which it has fulfilled right up to the present day, that of upholder and guardian of the financial system.

It is a curious fact of economic history that outbreaks of speculative fever, market collapses and financial scandals tend to happen at the end of major wars. The City of London learned this lesson in the years following 1713, when the long war with France was ended by the Treaty of Utrecht. The Treaty opened up fresh areas of the world, some of them very exotic, to British traders. In a wave of speculative fever, companies sprang up daily, promoting new ventures which would exploit these new possibilities. Some were genuine businesses, but many were totally fraudulent. One promoter even refused to state his company's intended area of business, merely asking for cash 'for carrying on an undertaking of great advantage, which shall in due time be revealed'. He managed to raise £2000 from gullible shareholders in just five hours – with which he vanished. Another promoter promised to discover the secret of perpetual motion. It has been estimated that during the boom some £300 million was subscribed to various companies.

The most prominent of these was the South Sea Company. This was granted the monopoly of trade in the newly-opened-up South Seas and promised fabulous returns to its investors. So fabulous indeed that its directors generously offered to take over and liquidate all the Government's debts. This was, of course, a threat to the Bank and its privileges. Alarmed at this challenge to its position, the Bank dismissed the offer. None the less, the new company received enormous political and public support, and its share price rocketed. At the beginning of 1720 its shares were trading at a few hundred pounds; by the end of June they were up to £2000.

In the autumn, however, the inevitable happened, and the South Sea Bubble broke. Numerous companies collapsed, and investors started questioning the soundness of the South Sea Company itself. In vain the directors promised a dividend of 30 per cent for the year, rising to 50 per cent the following year. Investors simply did not believe them and dumped stock. In desperation the Company turned to the Bank for help. Concerned at the impact such a collapse would have on the City, the Bank offered to support the South Sea

Company. This action says little for the good sense of the directors. In essence they were proposing to put a sound institution at risk in order to save a totally unsound one. Fortunately for the Bank this agreement could not be carried out, as the Bank was itself faced with a run on its deposits. This was met by resorting to various devices to slow the outflow of gold. Friends of the Bank jammed the counters to withdraw money, often in small coin, only to block the counters again in order to pay it back in. In the meantime supporters of the Bank raised fresh funds. Any thought of rescuing other companies was out of the question and the Bank was only able to save itself by abandoning the South Sea Company to its fate.

Anger at the promoters of so-called 'Bubble' companies was fierce. A parliamentary inquiry revealed considerable evidence of fraud and impropriety in the setting-up of the company. Stern action was called for and Parliament even passed a law, with harsh retrospective penalties, against 'the infamous practise of stock jobbing'. The search for scapegoats spared no one. The Chancellor of the Exchequer of the time, who had accepted payments from the Company, was expelled from the House of Commons and confined to the Tower. His property was confiscated to recompense victims of the collapse.

The South Sea Bubble crisis was a narrow escape for the Bank of England and one from which it emerged with a somewhat dented reputation. The episode had created an awkward dilemma for the Bank: in the event of a financial crisis, what was its role? Should it attempt rescues or not? And, if so, whom should the Bank be rescuing – investors, depositors or the banking system as a whole? These questions were raised every time there was a financial collapse, and remain a problem for the Bank of England.

Better years were to come. The more peaceful trading conditions in the decades that followed saw the Bank established on more secure foundations. It was still, however, a small institution in terms of staff and premises. When it opened it had only nineteen staff – including three cashiers and the Chief Cashier, ten tellers and two doorkeepers and messengers. Within a few months the number grew to over fifty.

The Bank's first offices were at the Mercers' Hall in Cheapside, but these were soon found to be inadequate. By the end of the first year the Bank had moved to more spacious accommodation in the

Grocers' Hall in Old Jewry. Unkind critics promptly nicknamed the Bank 'the Harpy of Grocers' Hall'. Everyone worked in one room: the essayist Joseph Addison, writing in the *Spectator* in 1701, noted, 'I looked into the great hall where the Bank is kept, and was not a little pleased to see the directors, secretaries and clerks ... ranged in their several stations according to the parts they hold in that just and regular economy.' The Bank only moved to its present position in Threadneedle Street in June 1734, though it was not until much later that it occupied the whole of the present-day site.

In those early days the Bank began creating its own traditions and jargon, many of which survive to the present day. The distinctive gatekeeper's uniform (now only worn on Thursdays – when the Court meets – and other special occasions) of 'a crimson cloth gowne lined with orange and a large bamboo cane with a silver head' dates from 1697. Much of the Bank's private language dates back centuries too. To insiders the Bank is the 'House', the staff list 'the House list'. The offices occupied by the Governor and directors are 'Parlours'. Holidays for staff are 'Governor's leave'.

The growing stability of the Bank was based on its perennial value to government. It was a virtuous circle: the Bank's shareholders, City merchants in the main, lent money to the Government to wage wars. These wars increased Britain's commercial influence and opened up new areas for trade, from which these same City merchants profited. The Government of course paid interest on these loans. But that was not the Bank's only source of income. Its note issue, a profitable business, was tied to government loans – the more money the Bank lent to the Government, the more notes it could issue. In essence this meant that every pound invested in the Bank earned its keep twice over. On top of all this there were the profits to be earned from discounting commercial bills, an activity of the Bank from its earliest days.

It was small wonder, then, when profit and patriotism could go so happily hand in hand, that new government loans undertaken by the Bank were swiftly subscribed. As the *Daily Gazetteer* put it in 1737, 'This flourishing and opulent company have upon every emergency cheerfully and readily supplied the necessities of the nation ... and it may very truly be said that they have in many critical and important conjunctures relieved this nation out of the greatest difficulties, if not absolutely saved it from ruin.'

15

Aside from the profits discussed above, there was a further price to be extracted for so readily supplying 'the necessities of the nation'. Each renewal of the Bank's charter – which tended to happen at times when the Government needed more money – led to further privileges. The renewal of 1709 had contained a clause making it illegal for any partnership of six or more people to enter the banking business, thus confirming the Bank's monopoly; and had confined to the Bank of England the right to issue notes payable on demand or with a maturity of less than six months.

By the mid eighteenth century the Bank was an important force in Britain. Indeed, it was seen as sufficiently established to merit the hostile attentions of the London mob – a potent force in the politics of the time. In 1780 there was a proposal to remove some of the restrictions under which English Catholics had laboured for almost a century. Opposition to the measure was led in Parliament by Lord George Gordon. Whipped up by his inflammatory speeches, the London mob took up the cause of anti-Catholicism and went on the rampage, attacking anything and anyone that could be construed as Catholic. The City authorities were reluctant to intervene to protect Catholics' lives and property and the mob was allowed free rein.

Encouraged by this official inactivity, the mob turned its attention to other targets. Newgate Prison was stormed and its inmates let free. Emboldened, the mob marched on the Bank of England, intending to sack it. Fortunately the Governor had some warning of this and put in hand defences which proved sufficient to deter the mob. Two rioters were killed directly opposite the main gate of the Bank, while several others were shot in Cheapside.

This episode is interesting for its consequences. The attack of the mob led to the establishment of a military guard on the Bank – each night an officer, three NCOs, a drummer (or piper) and twenty-four men, drawn from the regiment of the Brigade of Guards currently on duty in London, marched to the Bank and stood guard (in later years the number was reduced). Brigade standing orders note that the officer in charge was allowed a free dinner, to which he might invite 'one gentleman guest'. (Duties were taken very seriously. During the First World War, when members of the Honourable Artillery Company, a Territorial unit, found themselves on guard at the Bank, the Governor was refused admission

16

on the grounds of not giving the correct password. It is to the credit of the Governor that no reprimand was issued for this show of zeal.) The guard on the Bank remained for almost two centuries. It was abolished in 1973, and the job transferred to the Bank's own security force.

Shortly after this the Bank came under a rather more severe threat than that posed by the London mob. Its financial security was put at risk by the very circumstances that in earlier times had caused it to prosper. The war with France that broke out in 1793 proved itself a very different animal from those which had preceded it. It was, in many senses, the first total war of modern times – as much a conflict of economic systems and societies as a battle between rival armies and fleets. It was also, at £830 million, far and away more expensive than any before it. The National Debt rose during the revolutionary wars from £247 million to £861 million.

The demand that funding such huge sums placed on Britain's financial structure was enormous. The economy was hardly in good shape at the beginning of the conflict: the harvest of 1792 had been poor, and in November of that year alone no fewer than 105 business bankruptcies had been officially recorded. The strain of this was felt most by the country banks, local bankers who provided most of the credit used in business in the provinces. Many collapsed, and only the prompt issue by the Government of £5 million in Exchequer bills managed to shore up confidence and avert a general banking failure. For its part, the Bank increased its note issue to meet the demands of anxious customers.

But the real crisis came four years later, as the strains of war began to show. William Pitt, the Prime Minister, was a brilliant war leader; his financial skills, though, are less well known. He regarded Britain's economic power and wealth as essential weapons in the war with France. Cash was as much a weapon as a soldier's gun. In the early years of the war the British army was too small to intervene effectively on the Continent; so Pitt gave cash to Britain's would-be allies as a substitute for men. This led to a drain of bullion, which, combined with the rising cost of supporting an expanding war effort, put the Bank's resources under considerable strain. A report of the landing of a handful of French soldiers on British soil added to the air of crisis. The country banks provided the last straw. Their problems mounted as the war continued and by the end of 1796

17

almost a quarter of them had collapsed.

On 27 February 1797 the Bank was forced to suspend payment of cash for notes. That meant that Bank of England notes ceased to be convertible into gold. What could have become a major crisis was only averted by a statement from City merchants that they would happily accept Bank of England notes in payment of debts due and intended to settle their bills in the same way. More than 4000 people signed this declaration and their vote of confidence in the Bank seemed to do the trick. A run on the Bank was averted, and England settled down to living with a non-convertible paper currency for the duration of war. It was more than two decades before the Bank was able to resume payment on demand.

Had the population of England been reluctant to accept notes it might have been a different story (during the war France tried the same exercise and in so doing effectively destroyed the currency). As it was, inflation and the demands of war obliged the Bank to issue notes in lower denominations to meet demand; £1 and £2 notes were issued for the first time. Pitt's critics were scornful of the new paper, a result, as they saw it, of the Government's profligacy. Pitt's new notes were satirized by one wag of the time thus:

Of Augustus and Rome,
The poets still warble,
How he found it of brick,
And left it of marble.

So of Pitt and England,
Men say without vapour,
That he found it of gold,
And left it of paper.

Another critic of the time may have given the Bank its nickname: the playwright Richard Brinsley Sheridan, in a speech attacking Pitt's financial methods in the House of Commons, spoke of the Bank as 'an elderly lady in the City of great credit and long standing who had ... unfortunately fallen into bad company'.

Later writers were not so dismissive. Lord Stanhope, writing in Victorian times, saw the financing of the war as a triumph: 'it was', he wrote, 'a gigantic system of paper credit, giving us power to cope with no less gigantic foes'. Others have seen Pitt as the creator of many of the modern techniques of public financing using paper debt. But it was not a victory for paper alone: for standing behind the massive edifice of credit was the reality of a fast-growing economy. The Industrial Revolution was transforming Britain, and creating the wealth upon which the credit of the nation ultimately rested. Without the new industries that were to give Britain the dominant share of world trade in the nineteenth century, the war could never have been financed.

At the heart of Pitt's system of credit stood the Bank of England. It made the financing of the war possible, and shared happily in the growing prosperity of the nation, proving, yet again, that the cloud of war could have a very happy silver lining of profit. Even the stoppage of payment on notes did not damage the Bank's prosperity, and throughout the wars against France shareholders continued to receive dividends of 10 per cent.

It must be remembered that the Bank was just a private company, albeit one run with a judicious balance between public benefit and private profit. At the end of the war, the Bank's directors felt entitled to draw shareholders' attention to this and congratulate themselves on their role. In a resolution presented at a meeting of shareholders in May 1816 it was noted that 'the Honourable Court of Directors have acted with a degree of liberality and attention to the publick advantage, as far as was consistent with the duty and obligation they owed to their constituents'. The men assembled at the daily 'Books' meeting in the modern Bank are the latter-day inheritors of this 'attention to the publick advantage'.

2

'Watching the Gold'

The hundred years that separated the Napoleonic wars and the First World War could be seen as the heyday of the Bank. For the whole of the nineteenth century, Britain's financial system, with the Bank of England at its centre, dominated the world.

Yet any observer of the financial scene shortly after 1815 could be pardoned for thinking quite the opposite; all the signs suggested that yet again the system was on the verge of collapse. The end of the convertibility of notes into gold had led to a rise in the price of gold as confidence in notes had waned. Suspicion of paper money was so great that one landowner demanded payment of rent in gold rather than notes. And, just as had happened after the Treaty of Utrecht a century before, peace unleashed a wave of speculative fever. The euphoria of victory and a series of good harvests in four of the years after the battle of Waterloo created an atmosphere in which bubble companies flourished. Many were centred on the newly liberated countries of Latin America. The ending of Spanish rule and the creation of new states with a need for investment capital caused a rush of issues. It is estimated that in all £150 million was invested in ventures, many of them financially unsound, associated with South America. But that was not the only part of the globe to attract speculators. One enterprising businessman promoted a company to drain the Red Sea and recover the Egyptian treasure lost in the pursuit of the children of Israel. Faced with such activity the Bank's directors did not, for once, act with much prudence. Their initial reaction was to increase the note issue, an act which certainly encouraged speculative fever. Only late in the day did the

1. *James Gilray's cartoon 'Political Ravishment, or The Old Lady of Threadneedle Street in danger!' published in 1797.*

1a. *Montagu Norman, the Bank's longest-serving Governor, who served from 1920 to 1944.*

2. Top left: one of the earliest surviving Bank of England notes, dated 1699.

3. Top right: a country-bank note, issued in 1825 by the Andover Bank.

4. Left: one of the last of the Bank of England's famous white fivers.

5. In this box are the Bank's 'giants' – million-pound notes never issued to the public, but which back the Scottish and Irish banks' note issue.

Bank take the rather more traditional action of raising its discount rate to damp down speculation.

As in earlier crises, failure among the country banks was an important factor. These were an inherently unstable part of the system. The great nationwide clearing banks of today had not yet evolved – indeed, such enterprises were still illegal – and there were far too many tiny banks, each covering a very small area. One estimate suggests there were upwards of 470 country banks in existence in the first decade of the nineteenth century. Towns such as Abingdon, near Oxford, with a population of only 4500, had three. Many were run as a by-product of normal trade by local businessmen and their backing was minimal: the relationship between their note issue and the capital behind it was often non-existent.

Local businesses were heavily dependent on the bills issued by such banks. Any threat to a business or to its bank threatened the downfall of both. The result was that a small hiccough in the provision of credit could cause large-scale economic dislocation. In the wake of the speculative boom, many now collapsed. Critics contrasted the number of bank collapses in England with the many fewer failures in Scotland, and concluded that the legislation limiting the formation of joint-stock banks south of the border (passed as part of the Government's original deal with the Bank of England) was to blame – by limiting the number of partners a bank could have, the law effectively stopped the creation of big banks with a proper capital base and thus more stability. Proposals to change the law were vehemently resisted by the Bank. This was a somewhat short-sighted attitude: the Bank, rather in the manner of a medieval guild, protected its monopoly of banking with vigour, whilst simultaneously refusing to provide the branch network and national issuing of notes that would have remedied the weaknesses of the country banking system.

The crisis in country banking persuaded the politicians to override the Bank's views. In 1826 Parliament authorized the formation of banks with any number of partners, and with the power to issue notes, provided they were at least sixty-five miles from London. The Bank's response showed that it was, at heart, a commercially minded organization. It hastened to open branches around the country. The first such, at Gloucester, opened in July 1826. Within two years branches were opened at Manchester, Swansea, Birmingham, Liverpool, Bristol, Leeds and Exeter. Competition for business with country banks was vigorous – and resulted in some unpleasant incidents: Bank of England employees in Newcastle complained of dead cats and refuse being thrown over the wall of the Bank (presumably by rival bankers); others were paid danger money to move from London to open offices in the provinces.

It must be remembered that, while one part of the Bank of England operated as a provider of capital for the Government, another part acted as a normal retail banker, supplying banking services to customers. The emergence of potential rivals seemed to provide a spur to the Bank to provide better services. The system for drawing money from accounts, which had been somewhat Byzantine in its complexity, was made much simpler, and cheque books were introduced. The number of customers grew swiftly, and by the mid-1830s the Bank had almost 4000 accounts. Some remain customers to this day. In its new competitive image the Bank took on a business it had previously abandoned: mortgages. The great landowners of England were lent money on the security of their estates: the Duke of Rutland, for example, borrowed £300,000 at 4 per cent. But this business was soon stopped: as was pointed out, holding assets which might not be easily saleable had brought down many of the country banks.

In 1832 the Bank found itself again at the centre of the political stage. There had been considerable agitation throughout the country aimed at extending the very limited franchise to the middle classes of the new industrial towns. When the Duke of Wellington, regarded by many as the arch-enemy of this reform, became Prime Minister for the second time in May 1832, proponents of the extension of the franchise hit upon an ingenious way of removing him. The radical politician Francis Place came up with the simple slogan 'To stop the Duke, go for gold.' By this he meant cashing Bank of England notes for gold. (The restriction on converting banknotes into gold had been lifted a decade earlier.) It was a highly effective tactic: within days £1.25 million in gold had been withdrawn and the Bank was facing a crisis. The Duke conceded defeat: faced with the possibility of a financial collapse, on top of the threat of civil war and a turbulent House of Commons, he resigned on 15 May.

By the 1830s the Bank of England had evolved some way towards its modern position as a central bank at the heart of the financial system. It is clear from reading political diaries of the time that no government could have allowed the Bank to fail: as Wellington put it, 'the consequences would be ruin both at home and abroad'. Yet it was still a private bank, in competition with other banks. This competition was extended in 1833, with the removal of the ban on joint-stock banks in London itself.

None the less the stability of the Bank and the financial system was continually shaken during the Victorian era, just as it had been in earlier times. The crisis of 1839, for example, has a rather modern ring to it. It was caused by default on the part of a developing nation, and follows, in many respects, the pattern of the recent Third World debt crisis.

The country in default was the United States of America, which today has the most powerful economy in the world but was then a developing nation struggling to catch up with the advanced states of Western Europe. The United States had an enormous appetite for money to build the infrastructure that would open up its vast unexplored hinterland. Huge quantities of British capital were borrowed for this purpose. In 1839 several banks failed in America, and, three years later, two states – Maryland and Pennsylvania – defaulted (that is to say, suspended payments due on loans). Mississippi and Louisiana followed suit. City investors were outraged: the US financial agent in London was barred from his club in protest. Feelings ran so high that the clergyman Sidney Smith proposed a lunatic asylum for the American nation and asked how any Pennsylvanian could dare to sit down and eat at a table in London: 'he has no more right to eat with an honest man than a leper has to eat with clean men'.

Numerous British banks and finance houses found themselves in trouble as a result of the American defaults, and the Bank, fearful of the consequences of widespread collapse, eased the situation by advancing money against unpaid American bills. An agent of the Bank of England was despatched to the United States to renegotiate the terms of loans. Eventually most states resumed payment and all bar some £200,000 of the sums the Bank had advanced was recovered. But one state, Mississippi, never paid its debts and remains today technically in default.

The pivotal position of the Bank in the British financial system was becoming recognized – along with the need to separate its central-banking functions, notably note issue, from its commercial operations. In 1844 the Government, under Robert Peel, passed the Bank Charter Act, which still forms the basis of the Bank's day-to-day operations. The Act split the Banking Department and the Issue Department into separate entities, and limited the extent of the note issue.

A further aim of the Act was to eliminate note issue in England by banks other than the Bank of England, thereby removing one of the principal causes of instability in the system. Hundreds of country banks up and down England issued their own banknotes, failure to honour which all too often led to the failure of the bank issuing them. 72 joint-stock banks and 207 private banks had the right to issue notes at the time of the Act. Eliminating this privilege could be accomplished only gradually, as it was a profitable activity and any abolition of the right of issue could be seen as an attack on private property. The Act laid down that any private right of issue, once lapsed, passed to the Bank of England. Similarly, if any banking partnership had more than six members – a common state of affairs now that those banks could merge, beginning the process leading to today's clearing network – the right of issue passed to the Bank. The process of centralizing the issue took time – it was not until October 1921 that the last country bank to issue notes, Fox Fowler and Company of Wellington in Somerset, ceased to do so. None of this affected Scotland, where, to this day, right of note issue is retained by private banks.

Although this reform increased basic confidence in the currency, the strict controls on the size of the note issue laid down by the Act did not leave the Bank much latitude to increase it at times of public anxiety. Many critics believed the new Act would only serve to aggravate any time of difficulty. The crisis of 1847 illustrated their point. Brought on by a catastrophic failure of the harvest – especially in Ireland – and by a further outbreak of speculative mania (mainly in railway stocks), the threat of a run on the Bank was only averted by lifting the limit on note issue. The simple announcement by the Government that this would happen calmed nerves and stopped what could have been a dangerous crisis of confidence. But this was a weapon to be used with care: in 1857, when again the limit was lifted, the Government's letter to the Bank stated that 'Her Majesty's

Government rely upon the discretion and prudence of the directors for confining its operation within the strict limits of the exigencies of the case.'

At about the same time a further monetary weapon was brought to the forefront. One of the Bank's traditional controls over the money market had been its rate of discount: the amount it would discount on the purchase of acceptable commercial bills. From earliest times the power to vary the rate had been used as a control mechanism. However, after the passing of the 1844 Act the Bank decided to put the operation of its discount rate on a more formal basis. It was decided that the rate would in future be reviewed – and announced – weekly. This apparently cosmetic change had the beneficial effect of concentrating the mind of the market, and in time ensured that the Bank's rate of discount became the minimum rate at which money would be lent.

Before that, however, another change had been necessary to enable the discount market to operate effectively. Rates were still limited, in theory at least, by the medieval laws on usury. Since the time of Queen Anne the maximum rate had been set at 5 per cent, which inhibited the Bank's freedom to act decisively in times of financial crisis. Although in practice this limit was ignored, it was only after 1833 that the Bank was exempted from the operation of the usury laws.

The pre-eminence of the Bank in the financial system was now an acknowledged fact. This was a reflection of the position of the City in the world. London was, by the middle of the nineteenth century, the dominant centre for the financing of trade. Most of it was paid for in sterling, and bills of exchange drawn on London banks were universally acceptable. At the same time, allied markets, such as those in insurance and shipping, were centred in London. The City was also the main source of the world's capital for investment.

But despite the power of the City, and the growing influence of the Bank on the operations of London's markets, the second half of the nineteenth century saw a number of financial dramas. These are worth examining for the way in which they show the gradually evolving role of the Bank as guardian of the City's reputation. Bank insiders will tell you that it is a basic principle that firms which get into difficulties because of mismanagement will not be helped by the Bank; that it is no part of the Bank's duties to save people from the consequences of their own folly. That is a fine principle, as far as it goes. It becomes somewhat muddled when one comes to actual cases. For the Bank can find itself acting very differently when it comes to companies whose collapse, for whatever reason, would threaten the stability or good standing of the City. Two very different cases from this period illustrate this point. Both involved large and respected City businesses.

That of 1866 centred round the failure of one of the City's best-known names, Overend Gurney. This firm was engaged in money-broking in the City, and had dealt extensively with the Bank over more than thirty years. However, those running the firm in 1866 were not conducting its affairs in a very businesslike way: Walter Bagehot, describing the fall, said the partners made losses 'in a manner so reckless and so foolish that one would think a child who had lent money in the City of London would have lent it better'. The firm had gone into so many speculative businesses that failure, when it came, was on a large scale. On Thursday 10 May, Overend Gurney failed with liabilities of well over £5 million. The next day came to be known in the City as 'Black Friday'. The Bank declined to intervene directly on behalf of the firm, but had to take some action on behalf of the City as a whole. Financial panic was averted by massive advances by the Bank of England, coupled with the raising of the discount rate to 10 per cent. In addition the Government was persuaded to promise suspension of the limitation on note issue if requested. At no stage, however, did the Bank attempt to save the firm itself.

The other major crisis of the century also involved one of the City's best-known names – only in this case, because of the potential damage it would have done to the City's reputation, failure was regarded as an undesirable option. The Bank of England ensured that it did not happen.

The Baring Crisis of 1890 is still a phrase to conjure with in the Square Mile. But in a sense 'crisis' is the wrong word: although the problem was of considerable proportions and the amounts involved were huge, the troubles at Barings caused few ripples in the markets and were overcome surprisingly quickly. Barings Bank had been established in London in the eighteenth century by the brothers John and Francis Baring. Their father, Johann, was an immigrant from Bremen who had set up business in the cloth trade in Exeter in 1717. By the end of the century, the then Sir Francis Baring was said to be worth £7 million. During the nineteenth century Barings' wealth and influence grew – so much so that the firm was known, with Rothschilds, as the 'sixth power of Europe'. Barings' particular interest was in lending to the New World: the bank had raised large loans for the United States and had invested heavily in Latin America. It had run into trouble doing this in the past: Argentina had defaulted on its first loans in 1828, leaving Barings dangerously exposed. But over the years confidence returned and Barings became once more the leading bank in the Latin American lending business.

In the autumn of 1890 the bank had a huge accumulation of loans (principally Argentinian) which were effectively in default. By the beginning of November, the City was full of rumours that one of the great banking houses was in trouble. The news that Barings could not meet its obligations and might have to close within days presented Lord Lidderdale, the Governor of the Bank, with a dilemma. Barings' obligations were more than twice as large as the Bank of England's reserves, yet the failure of a bank as big as Barings would be unthinkable. What followed was a classic illustration of the unseen hand of the Bank at work.

Insiders in the City knew there must be trouble when Everard Hambro, a director of Hambros and of the Bank of England, was sighted in St Swithin's Lane at eight o'clock on a Saturday morning on his way to the Bank. The directors were meeting to determine what could be done. Little could be accomplished until a full statement of Barings' position had been drawn up. Lidderdale demanded this and thereafter acted with remarkable coolness, taking his son off to the zoo on the Sunday. On Monday morning he conferred with the Chancellor of the Exchequer. It was agreed that a committee of 'the great houses' (the big banking names) should be assembled and persuaded to give help. Meanwhile the Government would try and get Rothschilds to persuade the Bank of France to lend the Bank of England 'several millions' in gold.

By Wednesday morning Lidderdale had all the facts about Barings. It was clear that the bank was ultimately solvent, but that it might need as much as £8–9 million to meet immediate liabilities. This forced the Bank back into the hands of the Government. Lidderdale informed the Chancellor that he 'could not possibly go on with the matter at the Bank's sole risk' – that is to say, without guarantees from the Treasury. He got his guarantees in the form of a promise that the Government would bear half of any loss that might result from taking in Barings' bills during the next week. With this undertaking in his pocket Lidderdale set about raising enough City money to render it unnecessary. Within two hours he had promises of £3.25 million; within a day, almost £10 million, more than enough to keep Barings open. As a result the Government's guarantee never had to be called on.

The immediate crisis was over, although sorting out Barings took longer – after a lengthy liquidation over a four-year period, the business was reconstructed as a limited company. Every liability was met. The City was ecstatic. The Stock Exchange complimented Lord Lidderdale and the Bank Court on 'the masterly ability' with which they had averted a panic. Replying with modesty, the Governor expressed his pleasure at their belief that at 'a moment of danger I was able to do my duty'.

But not everyone joined the chorus of praise. The *Economist* magazine wondered if a dangerous precedent had been set. It suggested that the moral of the Baring Crisis was that a big finance house had in future only to over-commit itself 'to the extent of a sufficient number of millions' for rescue to be guaranteed. The magazine wondered if the certainty of being saved from the consequences of bad management would make for good banking practice in the future. This criticism has surfaced again in recent years, and on a similar subject: all too often modern banks have put themselves at risk by lending excessively to questionable borrowers.

One interesting aspect of the Baring Crisis was the large-scale involvement of the joint-stock banks. At one time the City bankers had looked down on them as larger versions of the despised and often unsound country banks. For their part the joint-stock banks resented being treated as country cousins by the grand bankers of the City. With justification they pointed to their financial muscle. With successive bank mergers and a generally rising level of prosperity, the joint-stock banks now commanded substantial deposits. The Baring Crisis offered them the chance to prove their value. When Lidderdale was seeking financial support from the City for the rescue, it was the joint-stock banks that offered most – their joint contribution exceeded that of the Bank and the private City banks.

The relationship between the Bank of England and the joint-stock banks had not always been so happy: to emphasize their power in an earlier crisis, one joint-stock banker was reputed to have remarked to a Bank official, 'I can draw a couple of cheques tomorrow morning which will shut you up at once.' The Bank Charter Act of 1844 had helped improve the relationship. By gradually removing the right of issue from country banks, one source of potential conflict had been removed. The Bank of England could concentrate itself on the highly profitable business of note issue, leaving the area of personal and commercial banking to the joint-stock banks. There were still areas of disagreement. When the Bank had raised its discount rate to 6 per cent during the Baring Crisis, the joint-stock banks had declined to follow suit, leaving their rate at $4\frac{1}{2}$ per cent. Lidderdale remarked plaintively that the Bank of England and the commercial banks were all in the same boat, but 'it would be for the common advantage of bankers and the country if the rowers would take their time a little better from the stroke oar'. It took some time for the Bank's authority on the subject of interest rates to be acknowledged.

Another key part of the Bank's modern position relative to the rest of the banking system came into being in the 1850s. There had been a long-running squabble between the joint-stock banks and the private banks over the clearing-house system (the means whereby payments between the various banks were settled). This was run by the private banks for their own benefit, and they saw no reason to allow the joint-stock banks to join. It was only when the latter threatened to set up their own system that a compromise was reached. Instead of settling accounts with each other in cash, all the banks agreed to payment by cheques drawn on their accounts at the Bank of England. This method continues to the present day.

From 1890 till the First World War the history of the Bank of England contained little of excitement – which is another way of saying that the system functioned happily with few crises. As one Chief Cashier of the time put it, 'the Bank was amazingly detached from international affairs; heard from no one, saw no one, only watched the gold and took the necessary steps automatically'.

The City did not exactly welcome the outbreak of war in 1914: it would disrupt trade, and threatened world financial stability. The Governor of the Bank, Walter Cunliffe, remarked to Lloyd George that 'the financial and trading interests in the City were totally opposed to our intervening in the war'. The immediate result of the declaration of war was predictable: a run on the Bank. Within a few days, the Bank had advanced £27 million, and reserves were down to less than half of that. Once again a letter of indemnity from the Government allowed the Bank to overcome the problem by increasing its issue of notes.

That done, the Bank turned to an urgent and traditional task: that of financing the war. By comparison with the final enormous cost of the war, the Bank's first advance to the Government, £6 million, was insignificant. It was soon clear that huge sums would need to be raised directly from the public. The first of many such war loans was raised in November 1914 and totalled £350 million at a rate of $3\frac{1}{2}$ per cent. Further loans later in the war raised almost £600 million and £950 million respectively. All these were managed by the Bank of England on behalf of the Government. Several other money-raising methods, such as war bonds and national savings certificates, were used also. But for the first time Britain found itself incapable of financing a war on its own, and money had to be borrowed from abroad, principally the United States. The stress of raising these sums while at the same time maintaining Britain's credit abroad led to a conflict between the Treasury and the Bank – a conflict that opened up the question of the control, and ultimately the ownership, of the Bank.

The details of the argument are complex and technical: suffice it to say that the then Governor of the Bank, a formidable autocrat called Walter Cunliffe (known with little affection as 'The Tyrant of the City'), got the Bank embroiled in an argument with the Treasury over who was in charge of the management of gold and foreign-exchange reserves. He acted in a somewhat high-handed way in the course of the dispute, and the Chancellor, Bonar Law, demanded that Cunliffe do as he was told. The argument was eventually brought to the notice of Lloyd George, by then Prime Minister. He decreed that Bank and Treasury should aim to work together, but that, in the event of a dispute, the views of the Government must prevail. The Bank was unwilling to accept this: the Committee of Treasury, effectively the board of executives of the Bank, informed the Government that it would be 'impossible for the Bank thus to renounce its functions'. In the end a compromise was arrived at, whereby the Bank agreed to confer with the Treasury 'before taking any action during the war involving the general conditions of national credit or substantially affecting the gold holding of the Bank'. Cunliffe managed to undermine this diminution of the Bank's authority by claiming that it did not affect the sole right of the Bank to manage interest rates. In the heat of war the dispute was left unresolved.

But many were now asking whether the peculiar situation of the Bank as a powerful private monopoly with enormous privileges could continue. Press criticism of the secretiveness of the Bank and the enormous power held by one man, the Governor, led to pressure for change. There were calls for the post of Governor to become much more akin to that of chief executive, reporting to the Committee of Treasury. Whatever was said, however, the office of Governor remained the centre of power at the Bank.

Peace brought some familiar problems and some new ones. (The traditional post-war fever of speculation did not reach its height till the twenties and culminated in the crash of 1929.) More immediately the Bank found itself facing the same problem as it had in 1815. During the war Britain had edged away from the gold standard: that is to say, the public had been discouraged – for patriotic reasons – from exercising the right to convert notes into gold at the Bank. A primary ambition of the post-war Bank was to see the full traditional convertibility restored as soon as possible. To the modern generation this desire must seem curious; those who have never lived with a currency backed by gold cannot really see why such a form of backing should matter. But, to a generation that had its ideas formulated by the long years of Victorian financial stability, the convertibility of paper notes was an article of faith, a principle of sound economics upon which the health of the nation rested. For the many the gold standard was synonymous with Britain's greatness.

But in reality it was not that easy to turn the clock back. In trying to get back to the gold standard, as the American economist J. K. Galbraith put it, 'the British followed the line of greatest resistance, causing great pain from the resulting self-inflicted wounds'. It did not look like that to the financiers of the time, or to Winston Churchill, who, as Chancellor of the Exchequer in 1925, triumphantly announced a return to the gold standard. In actual fact the return was less than wholesale, as no more gold coins would be minted – the action in practice meant only that gold would be available to pay for imports. The problem was that Churchill's advisers led him to fix the price of gold at the level it had been before the war. During the war sterling had depreciated heavily against gold and the dollar (a gold-backed currency). The effect of the decision was that British goods could only be competitive on the world market if their prices came down by about 10 per cent.

That was an uncomfortable prospect for a nation that was exhausted by war and had suffered severe economic dislocation and losses. Many British industries were in poor shape; investment had been at a low level and much-needed modernization had not taken place after the war. Many managers took an alternative route to lower costs – by cutting wages. This led to confrontation with the forces of organized labour. The General Strike of 1926 was precipitated by an attempt by the mine-owners to cut the wages of miners.

Although by no means the author of this policy of misery, the Bank had a hand in carrying it out. It was not alone in thinking that the comfortable times of earlier years could be re-created at the whim of a Chancellor. In pursuit of stability it urged the Government to reduce its swollen borrowing needs as soon as possible after the war. The Government was only too happy to oblige. Ignoring the expensive promises of 'a land fit for heroes' which had been made during the war, ministers hastened to reduce expenditure once peace had been declared. The result was widespread distress as the nation readjusted to much lower levels of government spending.

Behind the Bank's desire for a return to the gold standard was the conviction that this was the only means of restoring normality to international trade. This belief would have been fine if it had been shared by every other nation. Unfortunately it was not. Had the world economy grown rapidly, with little interference in markets, rates of exchange and trade, Britain might have exported its way out of trouble. As it was, wildly fluctuating exchange rates, combined with worldwide mismanagement of economies by governments (most of whom refused to take any steps towards liberalizing trade, let alone returning to a gold standard for international trade) resulted in a great deal of economic chaos. This made any revival of the stability of the pre-war years impossible.

Trying to persuade the rest of the world to behave like gentlemen was not helped by the actions of the victorious allies in ordering Germany to pay for the war. It was agreed in 1921 that the vast sum of £6600 million should be paid by Germany in reparations. To their credit the Germans tried to pay some of it off. Coal was sent to France and Belgium in lieu of money. This of course had the effect of putting French and Belgian miners out of work, not exactly what was intended. The inevitable result of this misguided attempt to make the loser pay for the war was the collapse of the German mark, which went into free fall against the other main currencies. At the beginning of 1923 there were already 80,000 marks to the pound; by September of that year, the figure was 19,000 million to the pound. Finally, after several further attempts to persuade Germany to pay up – including one scheme whereby the money to enable it to do so was advanced by those to whom it was owed – the notion of reparations was abandoned.

It was the Bank's good fortune during these difficult times to have one of the ablest figures in its history in the Governor's chair. Montagu Norman came from a distinguished banking family: his grandfather had been a director of the Bank for fifty years, and the banking firm of Brown Shipley was the family business. Norman was a remarkable-looking man with piercing eyes and a distinctive goatee beard, and what one friend described as 'a hopelessly Christ-like look'. He was austere in many of his habits – eschewing a chauffeur-driven car, he travelled to the Bank each day by tube (with his ticket tucked into the brim of his hat) – and he expected the nation to be equally careful with its money. Norman became Governor of the Bank in 1920, and, most unusually, held the job for more than two decades. During this time he put his stamp on the world's financial community and established an unrivalled reputation for skill and leadership.

Montagu Norman was at the centre of moves to re-establish economic confidence after the war. Behind the scenes he played a major role in rebuilding the shattered financial system of several European countries. In Austria, for example, under Norman's influence, a plan was introduced which halted inflation and stabilized the currency. It was a classic case of masterly yet scarcely visible pulling of the strings. But the reality of Britain's changed position in the world undermined Norman's best efforts. The war had been vastly expensive for Britain and the country owed almost £900 million to America. Britain's domination of world trade was at an end, and the British economy was now at the mercy of others. The Bank could no longer set a lead and expect the world to follow it unquestioningly.

The Great Crash of 1929 proved this beyond a doubt. Though it started in the United States, its effects were felt worldwide. The Americans found themselves learning the painful lessons that Britain had been taught after 1713 and 1815. During the 1920s steady economic growth had eventually developed into a speculative boom. This had led to an unprecedented rise in prices on Wall Street – a boom fuelled by the ready availability of money. During the twenties the amount of money devoted to trading on margins rose dramatically. It seemed that anyone could make money, and by the beginning of 1929 an estimated $5000 million was committed to margin trading by financial institutions, with another $400 million being added every month. The result was a surge in prices that bore no relationship to underlying values and earnings. A collapse was inevitable. When it happened, in October 1929, the savings of millions were wiped out. In just one week the value of 240 top securities declined by $16,000 million.

American businesses collapsed wholesale, to be followed shortly by many banks. Soon the rest of the world was affected too. Within two years Britain's exports fell virtually by half, and, as hundreds of businesses failed, thousands were thrown out of work. In time the crisis shook the financial system as well. In 1931 the Viennese bank Credit Anstaldt failed and a full-scale panic ensued across Europe. Even the Bank of England was shaken, with withdrawals of gold running at £2.5 million a day by the middle of July.

The crisis brought down the Labour Government of Ramsay Macdonald in August 1931, and a new National Government was formed, also under Macdonald. It determined to balance the budget and made massive cuts in public expenditure – cuts which were seen by many as cruel and heartless. The bankers carried the blame, but they too were faced with circumstances they could neither understand nor control. Within a very short time the bold post-war hopes of a return to the golden years of the Victorian age were abandoned. In September, the Government quietly went off the gold standard – the Bank of England's reserves were simply not large enough to sustain any form of convertibility. The gold standard never returned. The following year a further article of faith from Britain's heyday, free trade, vanished with the introduction of tariffs on certain imports.

For the bankers the thirties were as traumatic as they were for the rest of the world. In the United States, 1932 saw the failure of more than 2000 banks. Recovery was slow to come. The first signs were seen in 1935, and even then affected only a few industries. It was not until the rearmament of the late thirties that the slump lifted.

The advent of war in 1939 found the Bank at least rather better prepared than it had been for past wars. During Norman's governorship it had developed its role and grown in skill and stature. For the first time at the beginning of a war there was no financial panic. Machinery for controlling foreign exchange, originally devised in the First World War and improved during peacetime, was swiftly and effectively put to work. Firm controls on prices were implemented at once.

With the expensive lesson of the First World War in mind, Norman insisted that a policy of cheap money be pursued – indeed, interest rates stayed at 2 per cent throughout the war and for some years after. The result of this was that the financing of the war was much less of a burden than it had been in the past. Norman managed to persuade the people of Britain to lend money to the Government at 3 per cent, compared to the 6 per cent that had prevailed at the end of the First World War.

Norman's final and far-sighted bequest to the Bank and the country was the establishment of a committee to consider how best to meet the post-war financial needs of Britain, a sort of financial version of the Beveridge Report which helped create the Welfare State. This committee reported in the autumn of 1943. It accepted that many of the wartime controls would have to remain in place until the productive capacity of the economy had revived, and argued that low interest rates were essential to such a revival. On top of that the Bank was largely instrumental in creating organizations to provide the finance that would be needed by post-war industry. In May 1945 the Finance Corporation for Industry was created, to deal with the needs of larger firms, to be followed in July by the Industrial and Commercial Finance Corporation (better known as the ICFC), catering to smaller firms. Both were backed by the Bank of England and a number of the country's leading banks and insurance companies.

Ill-health, meanwhile, had forced Montagu Norman to end his remarkable period as Governor. Many saw his career at the Bank, though glittering, as a failure. His fervent belief in the need to return to the gold standard had collapsed in the face of the slump in the thirties; and he never saw fulfilled his dream of the City of London regaining its primacy among the world's financial markets. His greatest success was to make the Bank universally respected, if not liked. But this too could be seen, in a sense, as a failure. Norman's dream of a Bank that would dominate the domestic and international financial scene bore out the worst fears of one of his predecessors, Walter Cunliffe, who had remarked that if Norman ever became Governor it would end in the nationalization of the Bank.

Cunliffe meant this as a criticism; Norman saw public ownership as the almost inevitable result of the Bank's evolving role. He had put in hand measures which reduced the degree of competition between the commercial banks and the Bank of England; as he saw it, the Bank of England was now essentially a central bank and it was not the duty of a central bank to compete with high-street banks for customers. The pressure of war and financial crisis had inevitably pushed Bank and government into an ever-closer relationship; indeed, there had been criticism that the views of the Bank weighed too heavily in government thinking. Socialists in particular regarded the Bank as the spokesman for an international cabal of bankers, all aimed at halting the people's march towards the millennium.

In vain did Montagu Norman's successor as Governor, Lord Catto, try to dispel such views. In a speech celebrating the Bank's 250th anniversary Catto said, 'From time to time, the Bank is accused of having undue power. But neither the Bank nor any other body working for the Government can determine policy: the power to do that is the prerogative of Government and Parliament alone. What the Bank does is to give independent and candid advice based upon experience.' Such statements did little to dispel the view that the Bank was an *eminence grise*, exercising the real power behind the fiction of democratic government. The incoming Labour Government of 1945 had a long list of industries and businesses it wished to take into public ownership, and the Bank was firmly at the head of that list. As the socialists pointed out, central banks elsewhere were under the control of the state.

But, curiously enough, the actual act of nationalization, which took effect in February 1946, changed very little save the ownership of the Bank. As Labour's Chancellor of the Exchequer, Hugh Dalton, put it, it was 'a streamlined socialist statute, containing the minimum of legal rigmarole'. Streamlined socialism seemed to add up to the Bank being run just the same as before, with the difference that now the directors were appointed by the Crown on the advice of government. As Dalton explained in the second-reading debate on the Bank of England Bill, 'no day-to-day interference by the Government or Treasury with the ordinary work of the Bank was intended: that would be left, with confidence, to the Directors and their efficient and well trained staff'.

3

The Pound in your Pocket

If anyone can claim to have been the first to produce banknotes, it is probably that nation of ubiquitous inventors, the Chinese. The earliest recorded paper currency was issued in the seventh century by the T'ang dynasty. The idea appears to have been a success, as circulation of these notes continued for hundreds of years, and was only stopped in the fifteenth century under the Ming dynasty. The Venetian traveller Marco Polo records in 1298 'paper cut into pieces of money'. He describes it as having black lettering on a dark grey paper with a purple authorizing stamp: extraordinarily he does not mention the process by which it was produced, namely printing. Without printing it is, of course, very difficult to produce banknotes. For the essence of a banknote is that each one must be exactly like every other one.

Like so many Chinese inventions, the banknote and the techniques of printing on which it depended took time to come to the West. The first Western banknotes were issued in 1661 by the Bank of Sweden. Given the coinage which they were supplanting, it is hardly surprising that they were an immediate success. The coinage was based on copper, and as a result was somewhat inconvenient to use. The 10-dollar coin, for example, weighed, unbelievably, over 40 pounds. But the notes did not last long. They lacked the essential virtue of any paper money – public confidence. Demands to convert paper notes back into copper and a resultant outflow of copper forced the suspension of the note issue in 1664.

In England credit for producing the forerunners of today's bank-notes belongs to the goldsmiths, who had taken up the business of banking after Charles I's raid on the cash of London merchants stored at the Tower. When money was deposited with them, they issued receipts, which in turn tended to circulate as a form of currency. One eighteenth-century writer records that during the crisis of 1696, occasioned by the reminting of the coinage, 'all great dealings were transacted by tallies, bank bills and goldsmiths' notes'. The appalling state of the coinage by the later years of the seventeenth century – many coins were defaced or clipped – encouraged the use of paper notes. This was a point picked up by William Paterson in his proposal for a national bank.

Paterson suggested that the Bank should be allowed to circulate what he called 'Bills of Property'. In return the new corporation would undertake 'as a bank to exchange such current bills the better to give credit thereto, and make the said bills the better to circulate'. It is clear from this that he intended that the Bank of England should provide its own note issue. This issue, he believed, should be based on a backing of gold and silver bullion because 'everything else is only accounted valuable as compared with these'. But, seen from a modern perspective, he was far-sighted in wondering if this might always be so: 'All credit not found on the universal species of gold and silver is impracticable, and can never subsist neither safely nor long, at least till some other species of credit be found out and chosen by the trading part of mankind over and above or in lieu thereof.'

In practice, though, the Bank soon discovered 'some other species of credit'. It had originally been set up to lend all its own capital to the Government; in exchange it was granted the privilege of issuing notes backed by the security of these loans. There was no obvious logic behind this – especially given the rather poor record of governments when it came to paying back money that had been borrowed. It says something for the confidence generated by the new bank that almost from the start its notes were acceptable in commerce. But they were not legal tender – that is to say, money which if offered must be accepted in payment of a debt; nor did the founding directors of the Bank wish them to be: as one put it very perceptively, 'It's nothing makes bank bills current, but only because all those who desire it, can go when they will, and fetch their money for them.' In other words, it was realized that a banknote was only acceptable if those offered it in payment believed that they in turn could pay others with it, and that at the end of the day it would be honoured by the bank issuing it.

The first Bank of England paper note was similar in style to those of the goldsmiths. When a customer deposited money at the Bank, a receipt was issued, a note payable to the depositor or bearer. These early notes were entirely hand-written by a cashier, who inserted the total sum deposited at the Bank. These could then be presented at the Bank for payment in cash – gold and silver – in part or in whole. Such notes were of course mainly for odd amounts. The earliest Bank of England notes were thus somewhat like a modern building-society pass book; you could cash them in part for whatever sum you wanted when you wanted. Such notes circulated for almost a century. Fixed-sum notes took longer to arrive, but eventually became the standard instead.

A rather shorter-lived experiment was the interest-bearing note. These 'sealed bills' (so called because the Bank put its seal on them) carried interest on money deposited at 2d. per £100 per day. Though the Government accepted them as payment, they did not achieve a wide circulation. Those who used them regarded them more as a short-term investment than as a form of money. They were discontinued in 1701.

The issue of banknotes was an early priority of the Bank. On 31 July 1694, four days after the sealing of the Charter, the Court of Directors ordered that 'running cash notes be printed'. These were to be numbered notes in fixed denominations of £5, £10, £20, £50 and £100. Printed on them were to be the words 'We promise to pay Mr ... [payee's name and sum written in] at demand, London', with the date inserted again by hand. At the foot of the note was the message, still to be seen on today's notes: 'For the Govr. and Compa. of the Bank of England'. They were to bear the common seal of the company, the now familiar vignette of Britannia 'sitting and looking on a bank of money'. This idea was almost certainly borrowed from the portrait of Britannia commissioned by Charles II in 1667 – for which one of his mistresses provided the model – and which was in use in 1694 on halfpennies and farthings. Over the years the details of the design of Britannia have changed – on modern notes, for example, she looks to the left rather than to the right, as she did on some early notes. These first notes, however, seem to have been easy to forge and exist now only as proof plates:

40

it appears that they were never issued. The problem of producing a note that could not be forged was one the Bank was to face time and time again.

The next effort was little more promising. In 1695 12,000 notes were produced in various denominations; each denomination bore a large distinguishing letter. These lasted only a few months, as a forged £100 note was presented for payment in August of that year. The rest of the issue was hastily withdrawn. It seemed that without some form of security paper banknotes were doomed.

It took some time for the technology of paper-making to catch up with demand. The Bank knew the solution: paper with what it described as a 'mould' in it. By 1697 a way of inserting a distinctive watermark had been developed. The principle is intriguing: a wire mould in the design of the required watermark is laid into the frame and covered with the damp pulp. This ensures that the paper is thinner where it has laid on the wire pattern, and thus that, when dry, the design is seen clearly when held up to the light. One of the earliest surviving banknotes – which has a rather indistinct watermark – is dated 19 December 1699. It is $4\frac{1}{2} \times 7\frac{3}{4}$ inches in size, and is for the sum of £555, payable to Mr Thomas Powell. It was paid in three instalments. The sum, the name of the payee, the date and the clerk's signature are all in manuscript; the rest is printed. It was printed on a rolling copperplate press – basically a flat bed which passes between two round cylinders, all turned by hand. Such presses are now used for artist's engravings and the like. It was a slow process, with probably only four notes being produced every minute.

Attempts to produce a superior form of paper led the Bank into one of its longest commercial associations. In 1724 the Bank contracted Henry Portal, a paper-maker with a mill at Laverstoke in Hampshire, to produce high-quality security paper suitable for banknotes. To this day, Portal's is the Bank's paper-maker.

The new notes were still quite easy to forge, or alter. Indeed in 1722 the Bank took the unusual step of sending one of its cashiers to Newgate prison to talk to a forger who had been found guilty of altering one of the Bank's notes and was awaiting execution. The condemned man generously suggested various improvements to note design. The most celebrated forger of the eighteenth century was Charles Price, alias Old Patch. Price had the nerve to do some of his copying actually at a Bank counter. Despite a large reward it took the Bank a long time to track him down. Price was arrested in 1776 and, complaining of the tyranny of the action against him, took his own life in Bridewell prison.

It was in 1725, after Portal's new paper became available in quantity, that printing of notes in fixed denominations was resumed. But these were still payable to a specific person, and dated. As the number of notes in circulation increased, so the need to date them with the day of issue became somewhat academic, and during the eighteenth century this practice was dropped. The question of payee was more complex. Modern notes are payable to the bearer on demand; but the law in the eighteenth century was that a note so worded was not legally assignable to a third party, and was thus unacceptable as currency. To solve the problem the Bank made them payable to 'persons known to the Bank' (in time this came to be its Chief Cashier): this meant that whoever held the note knew that at any time it would be paid if presented at the Bank of England. For many years, Bank notes were nicknamed 'Abraham Newlands' after the man who was the Bank's Chief Cashier for twenty-five years. Newland's memory is still cherished at the Bank: a painting of him hangs behind the desk in the office of the Chief Cashier.

The highwayman also made his contribution to the evolution of the modern banknote. The robbing of mail coaches was a flourishing element of the eighteenth century's crime problem. It created a difficulty for the Bank in its attempts to create a currency that circulated freely: notes that were designed to be acceptable on sight could change hands into a highwayman's pocket as easily as anyone else's. One solution was the introduction of the post-dated bill. This was a form of money order payable three or, better, seven days after being presented at the Bank. This gave the aggrieved party time to stop payment if it had been stolen. A further security measure remains on notes to this day. Notes were numbered twice on the front – on the left-hand side and on the right. This meant they could be cut in two and sent by separate mails, to be joined up later.

Banknotes were only available in relatively large denominations till the middle of the wars against revolutionary France at the end of the eighteenth century. The Bank was reluctant to supply small notes, feeling that this need was best met by coinage and thus the Royal Mint.

Credit for the first £1 notes belongs to the Bank of Scotland. This had been established in 1695, a year after the Bank of England. Note issue being a highly profitable activity, the Bank of Scotland had hastened to produce its own notes. Other banks followed this example, and to this day three Scottish and three Northern Irish banks retain right of note issue. The Scots also learned a painful lesson from the forgers: when one £5 note had been altered to a £50 note by the deft hand of an artist, the Bank of Scotland resolved on different designs for the various denominations.

In 1704 the first Scottish pound note was issued: confusingly it read 'Twelve pounds Scots', then the equivalent of an English pound. With the abolition of the Scots currency as a result of the union in 1707, the notes became £1 notes. These have been retained in Scotland, although England ceased to issue £1 notes in 1984.

(In passing, this may be the place to settle a favourite pub argument – whether Scottish notes are legal tender in England and *vice versa*. The position is intriguingly complicated. Scottish notes are not legal tender in England; but, interestingly, neither are they in Scotland. Bank of England notes above the value of £1 – now of course the only notes issued by the Bank – are not legal tender in Scotland. £1 notes issued by the Bank of England were legal tender north of the border. This is because the modern £1 note was a descendant of the 'Bradbury' pound, issued in the First World War and so called after the then Permanent Secretary to the Treasury, who signed them. These were made legal tender throughout the United Kingdom. Any Royal Mint coinage is also legal tender in both England and Scotland. Before putting all these technicalities to the test, it is worth remembering the wise view of the founding directors of the Bank that it is a note's acceptability – that is to say, everyone's confidence in it – rather than its legal position, that gives it value. Legal tender is, it must be remembered, a rather tiresome and narrow concept.)

A further peculiarity of the Scottish note issue is worth mentioning here. Some readers may recall a slight but entertaining comedy called *The Million Pound Note*, made in 1954 and starring Gregory Peck and Wilfred Hyde White. The essence of the plot is that Gregory Peck is given a million pound note, which of course he cannot change. It thus becomes his passport to London society, where he lives a comfortable life on eternal credit, without ever parting with his million.

In this instance truth is almost as strange as fiction. The Bank of England does have million-pound notes, handsome creations printed in red ink on white paper. They look not dissimilar to the old white fiver and have, like every other note, the Bank's promise to pay and the Chief Cashier's signature. But these notes are never issued to the general public, and indeed never leave the Bank of England. They exist to back the Scottish and Irish banknote issue. In return for retaining the right of issue these banks are required to back that issue, pound for pound, with cash and securities held at the Bank in England. When a Scottish bank therefore wishes to increase its note issue by £1 million, it pays a cheque to the Bank of England and a million-pound note is formally issued, symbolically backing the extra Scottish notes. Someone in the Bank did once suggest that this quaint and rather literal practice might cease; legal advice was taken, and it was decreed that the law was unambiguous in requiring that the backing of the issue had to take the form of physical notes: and so the million-pound note survives. Notes for such large denominations are known in Bank jargon as 'giants'.

It has already been noted that the Napoleonic wars presented a challenge to the Bank and forced it to cease payment of cash for notes in 1797. Apart from being a blow to public confidence, this presented the Bank with a practical problem: if the economy was to keep going in wartime, and to do so without the benefit of gold and silver, a large new issue of paper currency had to be created. £1 and £2 notes were introduced in 1797; and they were needed in very great numbers. Large-scale production was not easy with the antiquated printing techniques of the time. Even so, by 1805 the Bank's printers, working flat out, were turning out 30,000 notes a day.

Each note was numbered, dated and countersigned by hand: a job which occupied dozens of people and ensured that each clerk could only process about 400 notes a day – and that meant a large staff. The introduction of a machine to print dates and numbers in 1808 increased productivity: they could produce 2000 notes in a day. But each note was still signed by hand until the latter part of the nineteenth century.

The increased production of notes, particularly of lower denominations, had the unwelcome result of a boom in forgery. £1 and
£2 notes were now circulating among people who had never seen
banknotes before, and thus did not know what they should look
like. For the next few decades the Bank fought a running battle with
the forgers. Each new technical improvement was soon matched by
an advance in the forger's art. The numbers of forged notes varied
from year to year: 1817, for example, was a bad year, with 31,000
forgeries detected.

In desperation the Bank turned to the public for help. Suggestions
were invited with the vague promise of a reward should any be
adopted: this proved an irresistible temptation for would-be inventors and eccentrics, who wrote in with a variety of outlandish
schemes. One correspondent proposed a system of inspectors on the
streets of London, whose opinion could be sought before any note
was accepted. Many proposed infallible and patent methods of
producing notes that would be impossible to forge. None were
successful: all too often the patient skills of the Bank's own engravers
proved that the method proposed could be copied only too easily.

What drove the Bank to such lengths was not simply dis-
satisfaction among its customers at being given forged notes. Uttering – that is to say, deliberately passing – a forged note was a capital
offence (as was forgery itself), and the number of executions was
becoming a matter of public concern. Between 1797 and 1829 an
estimated 618 persons were convicted, and most of them were
hanged. Public indignation was aroused by the fact that many of
those executed for uttering were merely the dupes of the forgers,
few of whom were ever caught. The Bank was seen as the sinister
force behind this spate of prosecutions: one contemporary magazine
described the Bank's directors as 'grand purveyors to the gibbet',
and in a macabre sketch of 1819 George Cruikshank portrayed on
a mock banknote the sufferings of those condemned under the
forgery law. Such public disquiet eventually led to the abolition of
the death penalty for forgery in 1832.

It took the Bank many years to produce notes that could not be
forged easily. The magnitude of the problem can be seen from the
distinguished list of experts on whom the Bank called for help. At
various times Michael Faraday the physicist, Charles Babbage the
mathematician, Marc Isambard Brunel (father of the famous Isam-

bard Kingdom Brunel) and Joshua Field, founder of the Institution of Civil Engineers, were consulted. Even Parliament was mobilized: in 1801 use of a wavy watermark in paper, recently introduced into banknotes, was restricted by law to the Bank.

Numerous attempts were made to produce a design that could not be copied; but that in itself produced a problem. The wear on printing plates meant that, to meet the demand for notes, any design had to be capable of being copied many times inside the Bank. This meant that proposals for fine-art designs to be included in notes had to be abandoned. In truth the state of printing and paper technology was not sufficiently advanced to beat the forger.

The Bank found another solution to the problem. In 1821 stocks of gold were sufficiently high for cash payments to be resumed. This led to the withdrawal of £1 and £2 notes, the ones that had been most forged. The lowest-denomination Bank of England note was once again £5.

But ironically technology now came to the aid of the Bank. The introduction of a new steam-driven printing press in 1836 was a major step forward. This had been devised by John Oldham, the chief engineer and engraver to the Bank of Ireland. It was capable of producing much larger numbers of high-quality notes. More important, it was capable of numbering them sequentially, starting at 00001 with a cypher or code letter in front. Each print run could thus have its own code, a potential trap for the forger. At the same time it was decided to include in the design of banknotes no fewer than five different methods of engraving. It was hoped that this would deter even the most skilled forger.

One commonly suggested improvement over the years had been the adoption of a habit of the country banks issuing notes. Many of these included little scenes in their note design – illustrations of local landmarks and the like. Unfortunately, though these made for a pretty note, they did not actually make it worth anything. Customers fell into the trap of believing that a well-produced note was a sound one. In too many cases the beautiful note proved a worthless commodity when the bank issuing it failed. One anonymous victim of this remarked that 'any adventuring swindler, who could afford to pay for the engraving of a copper plate, set up a bank'. Many country banks did not seem to think it their business to worry what backed their issue, and accordingly put a lot of effort into securing a wide circulation for their notes regardless of the consequences: one indignant director of the Bank reported, 'on market days they employed persons to go out and ... withdraw from circulation all the paper of the Bank of England and substitute for it their own'.

The situation in which Bank of England notes were treated like any other despite their superior backing and general acceptability was highly unsatisfactory. The first tentative step towards giving them a real status was taken in 1833, when Bank of England notes were deemed by Act of Parliament to be legal tender – although certain restrictions were placed on this. Repeated proposals to confine to the Bank the right of note issue – to make it, in effect, an issuing central bank – were resisted with vigour. The country bankers' committee complained in 1833, 'Should this great corporation, conducted by directors who are not personally responsible, become the entire dispensers of the circulation of the country, and supplant the existing banking establishments – they will then be able to contract or expand the currency according to their separate and particular interests and convenience, and thus be armed with a power and influence dangerous to the welfare of the community.'

The 1844 Bank Charter Act settled that argument by separating the Bank's Banking and Issue Departments and effectively limiting the right of issue to the Bank of England – albeit over a long period. The Act also obliged the Bank to redeem notes for gold at a fixed price. This decision derived from the old theory that a currency required a gold backing: in reality the backing for the currency was beginning to move away from gold. The stringent rules for note issue laid down in the Act – that it be backed by securities up to a certain level, and by gold thereafter – soon proved unworkable. The significance of this was not seen for a long time.

In effect, what was happening was that physical money was ceasing to be of paramount importance in the conduct of economic life. Increasingly transfers, by means of cheques, between commercial-bank deposits were supplanting cash and notes. Gold continued to play a part – albeit increasingly insignificant – in the real-life economy until the First World War. Then, in an effort to conserve gold stocks, the public was encouraged to pay gold coins in and draw notes out instead. By 1916 gold coins had effectively stopped circulating, though many remained in private hands. The Cunliffe Committee, set up to consider currency and foreign exchange after the war, suggested in 1918 that gold should not be allowed back into the hands of the public on any large scale: 'people have now become fully accustomed to the use of notes and it is probable that . . . they will continue to circulate instead of gold coin much as they do at present'. Within a relatively short space of time gold was, in the words of one historian, Emmanuel Coppieters, 'relegated to a mere commodity reserve for the settlement of international accounts'.

It took longer for the powerful ban on increasing the note issue, imposed in 1844, to be removed. This limitation on the note issue was seen by nineteenth-century economists as essential to maintaining confidence in the economy. The 1928 Currency and Bank Notes Act limited the Bank's fiduciary issue (that is to say, the part of the issue backed by government and other securities as opposed to gold) to £260 million. On the outbreak of the Second World War, the limit on the fiduciary issue was effectively scrapped. The lack of importance of this was shown by the fact that, despite a doubling of the note issue during the war, there was no noticeable inflationary effect.

During the war, large-denomination notes of £10 and over were withdrawn from circulation. The Chancellor of the Exchequer explained that this would 'provide an additional handicap for those who may contemplate breaches of exchange control and other regulations'. During the war, the best-known of all English notes, the famous white £5 note, also came under threat, albeit from a different direction. The Germans attempted to undermine the stability of British currency by printing a vast number of forged notes. With the resources of a government behind them, they were good forgeries; but they failed in their intention because of another act of wartime monetary control in the UK. The import of Bank of England notes was banned to ensure that Germany did not receive any benefit from the stocks of British currency taken when European countries were overrun by its armies. This act effectively stopped the Nazis from introducing the fine product of their forgers into Britain.

Ever since the heyday of the forgers in the early nineteenth century the Bank had been reluctant to give them opportunities by issuing notes for small denominations. While notes for £1 and £2 had been in circulation, the battle to prevent forgeries had been expensive and defeat had eventually been conceded: in 1821, when the Bank withdrew its small-denomination notes, it calculated that some £40,000, a huge sum in those days, had been spent on the attempt to produce an unforgeable note. In addition the Bank had been left with a large stock of unusable notes.

In 1891 the then Chancellor of the Exchequer, George Goschen, proposed the issuing of £1 and £2 notes as a means of boosting the gold reserve. If more gold could be kept in banks, where he felt it belonged, rather than the nation's pockets, a larger sum would be available to meet financial crises – during the Baring Crisis of the year before, the Bank of England had been forced to call on the Bank of France for gold because its own reserves were inadequate. But Goschen's proposal did not find favour with the Bank's directors, still scarred by the experience of their battle with the forgers.

The call for small-denomination notes was met in the First World War by the Treasury rather than the Bank, with the issue of 'Bradburys', discussed earlier. Millions of these were produced during the war, and by the time peace arrived they were an accepted part of the currency. The Bank's aversion to small notes was not overcome till 1928, when the Bank's artists produced satisfactory designs for £1 and 10s. notes. These were issued on 22 November 1928, and notes for these denominations remained in circulation until recent times.

It is interesting to note that the British monarchy only made its first appearance on a Bank of England note – in the form of the Queen's head on the £1 note – in 1960. The Bank has made up for this rather belated gesture to the Crown by retaining on its notes to this day the portrait of the Queen used on that first note. This creates a delicate diplomatic problem for the Bank's designers: will they, at some stage, allow the monarch to grow old gracefully, or should she, like Britannia, remain ageless to the Bank?

It seems one of the rules of currency that anything new is disliked, however much people once hated that which has been replaced. Thus the demise of the once-despised £1 note in 1984, and its replacement by a coin, was greeted with dismay. One Member of Parliament described the decision as 'symbolically, very bad'. Symbolism, however, had to give way to the realities of production: although each pound note cost only $1\frac{1}{2}$ p. to make, its life expectancy was barely ten months. The new pound coin, by contrast, costs $2\frac{1}{2}$ p.

to make, but should last for forty years.

Today the Bank produces £5, £10, £20 and £50 notes. The design still incorporates much of the wording of its first banknotes, despite the many changes in the nature of notes since 1694, and includes the promise to pay. The *Penguin Dictionary of Commerce* defines a banknote as 'a piece of paper purporting to pay the bearer on demand a specified sum of money in gold and silver coin'. The key word is 'purporting', because of course the banknote is in a sense an act of faith on the part of those who handle it: it is worth what it says because you and others believe it to be worth that. As for the promise to pay, if you presented a £10 note at the Bank of England and demanded payment, they would look at you in some surprise and hand you another £10 note or perhaps two £5 notes, or ten £1 coins.

The size of the modern note issue, which so much vexed the Victorians, is determined by the market: if customers want more notes, the Bank prints and issues them. In effect this means that the issue rises at about the same rate as inflation; and the most recent Act regulating the issue leaves the matter of its volume largely to the discretion of the Bank. In order to prevent the Bank from repeatedly asking the Treasury's permission for an increase, the level is reset from time to time, but always comfortably above the normal level of issue. But a legacy of a century ago does survive. Each week, in accordance with the Bank Charter Act of 1844, the Bank of England produces a statement of position of the Banking and Issue Departments. That of 8 October 1986, for example, showed notes for £12,583,967,354 in issue, with a further £6,032,646 held in the Banking Department. Against this is the backing to the issue, £12,590 million of government debt, other government securities and acceptable commercial bills. The exercise is a quaint one, with little significance, but, like so many other rituals at the Bank, one carried out with care and precision.

Overseeing the note issue, once a matter of survival, is today an exercise in production management allied to knowledge of the market. The banking system needs notes on a Friday – both for those workers who are still paid in cash and to meet the demand for weekend shopping. On Mondays, by contrast, notes flow in: mainly from traders banking the weekend's takings. At certain times of the year, such as Christmas, there is an enormous growth in the note issue: the issue in the weeks immediately before Christmas 1985, for example, shot up by almost £2000 million. Most of that, of course, returned to the Bank in due course.

The new technology of banking has added to the Bank of England's headaches, in the form of the widespread adoption of cash-dispensers by the banks and building societies. Cash-dispensers eliminate customer waiting time and save on expensive cashiers – good news for the banks and building societies. But the new machines are creating a problem for the Bank of England: many of them reject anything but brand-new notes, which shortens the average life of notes. Although newer machines are less finicking and will accept used notes, damaged and creased notes can jam them. The Bank has been forced into an expensive investment programme installing machines that will check returned notes. New sorting machines have been introduced, each of which can process 300,000 used notes a day. Approximately half are passed for reissue, the other half being destroyed. At the same time these machines are capable of rejecting what the Bank quaintly calls 'foreign' notes (mainly Scottish and Irish ones) and other bits of paper which creep into the banking system: private cheques and luncheon vouchers frequently find their way into the heaps of notes returned by retailers.

At one time all banknote printing was done – literally – in house at the Bank in Threadneedle Street. But, as demand for notes grew and printing equipment became more sophisticated, the operation was moved to separate premises, first in Old Street, and then to the outskirts of London, in Essex. Vast numbers of new notes are produced every year. In the year ending February 1986, 1187 million notes of various denominations were produced there. (About the same number are destroyed every year too.) This makes the Bank a large employer of industrial labour: more than a quarter of the staff work in the printing works. The demise of the £1 note has eased the pressure and resulted in the loss of approximately 300 jobs at the printing works.

The design of notes is a job in which the Bank takes great and justifiable pride. Each new note design involves months of research and drawing. Every ten years or so, a new series of notes is introduced. The current series has well-known Britons on it, together with illustrations of their achievements. The £50 note, for example, which features Sir Christopher Wren, is incredibly intricate in its design. It includes detailed drawings of St Paul's Cathedral – and even the background geometric design on the note is taken from Wren's decoration inside the cathedral. An important priority is ensuring that it cannot be copied: this involves very careful choices of colours – up to fifty different ones in some cases. But even so the designer can put his own mark on a note: if you have a microscope it is worth seeing if you can spot the designer's private joke on the back of the £50 note – in among the crowded details of the view of London from the Thames is a dog taking a boat ride!

The massive numbers of notes produced every year make the Bank of England the most consistently successful nationalized industry in the country. Few businesses have a monopoly in making a product everyone has to use, a monopoly protected by Parliament; fewer still can make that product for a few pence and then sell it for £10 or even £50. In the old days those profits went to the shareholders of the Bank. Nowadays, under public ownership, all the profits of note issue go to the Treasury. It is a handy bonus for the taxpayer: profits in the year ended February 1986 were £1,396,757,000. Not that it is recorded in the Bank's accounts as anything so sordid. Against that figure is the simple statement 'Payable to the Treasury'.

The Victorian economist David Ricardo would have approved: indeed, this was what he suggested as far back as 1824: 'the commerce of the country would not be in the least impeded by depriving the Bank of England of the power of issuing paper money ... the sole effect of depriving the Bank of this privilege would be to transfer the profit which accrues from the interest of the money so issued from Bank to Government'. But it is worth recalling that without the profits of note issue the Bank, as a private institution, would have not been able to continue for so long its role as upholder of the financial system.

6. *Bank printing works. Old notes which cannot be reissued are burned: this is £6 million worth of £5 notes going up in smoke.*

7. *Bank printing works. Newly printed notes being checked.*

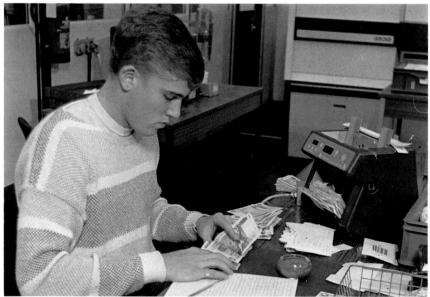

8. *Bank printing works. Notes being sorted before reissue to eliminate 'foreign' ones – that is, Scottish notes.*

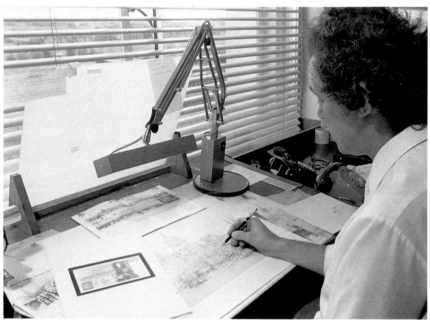

9. *Bank printing works. Roger Withington, artist-designer, working on detail of the design of the £50 note.*

10. *A face to match a well-known signature: Chief Cashier to the Bank, David Somerset, seated under a portrait of one of his most famous predecessors, Abraham Newland.*

11. The gold vaults of the Bank lie far below street level at Threadneedle Street.

4

Excuse me, Chancellor ...

Once upon a time bank-managers used to be rather tiresome people, with a habit of telling the rest of us how we should live our lives, and what we should spend – or, more likely, not spend – our money on. They were that niggling voice of conscience, urging the virtues of thrift and prudence. Casting a baleful eye over our financial health, they urged us to spend only what we had earned, and not to undertake commitments we could not afford.

Nowadays all that has changed. Today's bank-manager is more likely to sell us a new credit card or life-insurance policy, or plead with us to borrow more of his bank's money on an unsecured loan. Competition among banks for business has turned bank-managers from being pillars of fiscal caution into something more like door-to-door salesmen.

But one has stood out against this trend – one who does not face any competition for business. The nation's bank-manager, if one can call the Governor of the Bank that, is still like the old-fashioned ones used to be.

Speaking at the Mansion House dinner for the bankers and merchants of London in October 1986, the Governor, Robin Leigh-Pemberton, warned the nation of the consequences of excessive pay rises: 'Our performance to date on productivity comes nowhere near to warranting the 4–5 per cent annual growth in real incomes ... [Although] room does exist for some rise in living standards, we should not forget past experience of too rapid a rise in consumption all too easily leading to growing trade deficits. Part of the solution must be a sharp reduction in the general level of pay settlements.'

These strictures were not aimed at the long tables stretching away in front of the Governor: the aristocracy of the City do not see themselves as being included in anything as vulgar as pay restraint. The target for the Governor's remarks was rather closer to hand – the Chancellor of the Exchequer, Nigel Lawson, and his team of ministers seated at the top table. Through them he was delivering a traditional lecture to the nation at large. The Bank's view was that, yet again, the level of pay settlements in Britain seemed to bear no relation to the rise in prices or productivity. It is not a new thought. Mr Leigh-Pemberton's comments could have been lifted wholesale from almost any earlier speech by any Governor of the Bank.

The evolution of the Bank to its modern position as the nation's bank-manager and financial conscience has been a slow process, complicated by the ways in which the Bank has had to come to terms with politics and politicians – and they with it. It could be compared to a dance with three participants, Bank, government and Parliament. Two of these participants, Bank and government, have, over the years, worked out their own dance routine (though there have been times at which they have trodden on each other's feet); the third party, Parliament, is suspicious of this private little dance and would like to join in. Neither of the first two partners wants anyone cutting in on them, so they discreetly resist the interloper. Every time Parliament has sought some control over the relationship, or even some information about it, the other two parties have joined forces to keep it at arm's length.

In the early days Bank and government were by no means equal partners. Banking was not seen as an honourable profession: the historian Clarendon, in a famous phrase, described bankers with aristocratic disdain as 'a tribe that had risen and grown up in Cromwell's time, and were never heard of before the late troubles'. The original directors of the Bank were seen by some in government as little better than the despised goldsmiths – at best as a higher class of usurer, and certainly hardly an equal. As a result the tenor of early communications between government and Bank tended on the side of government to haughty disdain and command, and on the side of the Bank to subservient hand-wringing.

But to shrewder minds the mutual interdependence of Bank and government was clear from the start. Thus in 1697 Charles Montagu, the Chancellor of the Exchequer, writing to a fellow Cabinet minister, acknowledged that this was the essence of the relationship: 'the Bank notwithstanding all the hardships and discountenance they have met with are yet resolved to venture all for the Government and I hope what they do in our distress will not be forgotten in theirs if ever they are in a greater'. (Not for nothing is a portrait of Montagu accorded a place of honour in the Bank's Court Room.)

Parliament has a long tradition of being suspicious of the Bank of England, starting from the debate on setting up the Bank in 1694. The Commons, exhausted at the King's insistent demands for cash, passed the Act establishing the Bank almost on the nod. In the Lords it was a different matter. Many were worried at control of money passing out of the hands of Parliament. As a contemporary diarist put it, several peers 'brought forth a number of arguments to show that it would be injurious to the King, since it was not to his interest that the management of such large funds should be in other hands than those of the Government'. The Bill eventually became law, by a mere twelve votes, only because the Lords were reluctant to precipitate a conflict with the Commons over money. None the less, a clause was included which prohibited the Government from raising money via the Bank without the consent of Parliament.

Part of the problem was that the Bank was clearly viewed as the creation of one political party. Its promoters and investors were all prominent Whigs, who had a vested interest in war and the resulting expansion of trade. The Tories thus took every opportunity of criticizing and undermining the Bank. In 1710 the directors of the Bank were so bold as to send a deputation to Queen Anne complaining of the numerous changes she was making in her government. Such changes, they said, were upsetting the markets. The Queen indignantly dismissed such complaints as 'monied impertinence'. The Tory Press was beside itself with rage: one newspaper printed a 'Loyal Address' to the Queen purportedly from 'your majesty's most audacious, imperious, directing and commanding subjects', meaning the Bank of England. The Tories' next tactic was an attempt to seize control of the Bank. A group was formed to try and take it over – what in modern Stock Exchange parlance would be called a concert party. They were rebuffed at a hard-fought meeting of the proprietors in 1711: one Tory protagonist, the celebrated Dr Sacheverell, was reportedly 'hissed at in the Bank'.

Eventually politicians of all shades came to accept that the Bank was a useful fact of life.

Dealings between Whitehall and the Bank have always relied heavily on informality and personal relationships. This too dates from the early years and is nicely summed up by the career of one man, William Lowndes. It was through his good offices that the Bank was able to build up its position and a relationship with government. Lowndes was Secretary to the Treasury – that is to say, the permanent head of the Treasury – from 1695 until his death in 1724. But that was not his only role: the rather easy-going customs of the time enabled him to be a Member of Parliament and a holder of Bank stock at the same time. He was consulted about impending legislation and twice introduced to Parliament measures that benefited the Bank. At the same time, as head of the Treasury, he could be relied upon to sort out any problems that might arise in the Bank's day-to-day relations with government. Any modern Sir Humphrey would be green with envy at the power of this eighteenth-century mandarin.

Sheer administrative convenience – the need for banking services – played a part in the growing relationship of government and Bank. At an early stage the Government declared that it would regard the Bank's bills as an acceptable form of payment. In return the Bank, albeit with some reluctance, accepted bills drawn on the Exchequer. (The reluctance was due to the fact that many of the smaller bills competed with the Bank's own notes.) In time Exchequer bills were cashed, deposited and accepted as security at the Bank. The Bank also came to handle the management of the National Debt by the middle of the eighteenth century. In addition it soon became the custom for heads of various government departments to borrow short-term money from the Bank to meet specific payments. It became standard practice for the Bank to advance money to various government officials against the security of future income.

Interestingly, most of these early government accounts were in the personal name of the office-holders. In the 1740s for example, William Pitt the elder seems to have had a very active and large account in his own name at the Bank: but this merely reflected his position as Paymaster-General to the Forces. It seems that no one ever actually issued instructions that departments of state should keep their accounts at the Bank, but over the eighteenth century this became the norm.

Proposing the renewal of the Charter in 1781, the Prime Minister, Lord North, described the Bank as 'to all important purposes the public exchequer'. That this was so was not entirely unrelated to the extraordinary inefficiency of the Exchequer. Never the best-run department of state, the Exchequer relied right the way through the century on medieval practices and technology: for example, the system of tallies (sticks with notches cut into them as a record of debts and payments) was still in use. The office of tally-cutter was abolished in the reign of George III – though to protect the interests of the holder the abolition was not to take effect till his death. Unfortunately for the reformers, the tally-cutter proved to be a man of great good health and longevity. Such practices made it inevitable that government departments should prefer to handle their receipts and payments through the Bank of England.

In the same speech Lord North described the Bank, somewhat excessively, as 'from long habit and usage of many years ... part of the constitution'. This piece of hyperbole was not unrelated to the fact that his government was chronically short of money, and his speech was part of a debate on the renewal of the Bank's charter in return for further loans. The suspicions of Parliament were aroused. Members felt that the Bank, with the Government over a barrel, was driving too hard a bargain. Lord North was urged to look elsewhere for money: let him, said one critic, 'go a shopping with the maids of honour, till he has learnt that the best way to make a bargain is by going to more shops than one'.

But Lord North got his way and the 'shop' its new charter: the relationship was simply too convenient to allow parliamentary ructions to threaten it. The Bank, however, was by no means insensitive to the views of Parliament: in 1778, the directors wrote to the Government about their worries at the large numbers of securities being presented at the Bank for payment which were not covered by parliamentary votes – the Bank did not want to appear to be flouting the terms of its charter.

As has been noted, the Napoleonic wars confirmed the central position of the Bank in the finances of the state. Despite frequent battles between the directors and the Government – over the fees charged to the Government and the amount of government paper

57

presented at the Bank – both sides knew that they needed each other in order to sustain the business of waging a war. One conflict in particular showed that there was a moral gap between the attitudes of bankers and politicians to money.

In 1789 the Prime Minister, Pitt, discovered from an inspection of the Exchequer and Audit rolls of the Bank that the balance of unclaimed dividends due on government securities held by the Bank was increasing. He proposed to raid these balances for 'the temporary use of the public'. This did not impress the directors of the Bank: they knew precisely what a politician meant when he used the word 'temporary'. When Pitt threatened the Bank with an Act of Parliament, the Bank responded with a warning that 'the Bank will probably find it necessary in some way to bring [the matter] before the public eye'. The threat of a public attack on government policies by the Bank was – and remains to this day – an important weapon, albeit one that has never really been used. In the event both sides backed down from open confrontation and a compromise solution was found.

By the 1830s the Bank of England was most of the way towards its role as central banker to the state. But important parts of the Bank's modern duties had not yet developed. Its role in minding the exchange rate and money markets and acting as a part of the process of government policy formulation did not come for another century. That was because public management of such matters did not seem appropriate to the Victorian world: despite the financial crises of the century, few felt that the state had any duty to manage markets. As the mid-Victorian Prime Minister Robert Peel put it, the Bank was just like any other 'banking ship'; it was adrift on the sea and unable to control market rates. This made for a somewhat passive role for the Bank, enabling it to steer well clear of political issues, and act only in its straightforward role as banker to the state.

Maintaining that role was quite easy in the days when the governing class was a small elite of like-minded people, essentially the same group as that dominating the business world. On the whole there was little chance of the Bank and Government falling out on matters of policy: both were pursuing similar ends and it was quite possible for a man to have interests which overlapped finance and politics. (George Goschen, for example, served for many years as a director of the Bank and then switched to politics, ending up as Chancellor of the Exchequer.)

As in so much else, the First World War changed this comfortable state of affairs. Under the pressures of total war the ambiguities in the relationship with the Treasury were forced into the open. The battle between the Government and the Bank over who was responsible for the management of foreign-exchange reserves was the watershed. Lord Beaverbrook, in a letter to *The Times* in 1955, claimed that Governor Cunliffe's row with the Chancellor of the day, Bonar Law, 'destroyed the independent authority of the Bank and established for the first time the ascendancy of the Treasury ... it was the turning point in the Treasury's relations with the Bank. In fact it was the beginning of nationalization.'

The war also saw the ending of nineteenth-century *laissez-faire* attitudes, with large-scale state involvement in the running of the economy for the first time. It was widely expected that this would cease with the end of the war. But the hardly less turbulent years of peace saw little reduction in the role of the state. At the same time the growth of democratic political influences and attitudes meant that the old cosy and informal relationship between government and Bank came under more public scrutiny.

One would have expected the conflicts to be worst with Labour governments: they, after all, were committed to a radical change in the balance of economic power. Certainly the markets thought so: the prospect of a Labour government emerging after the 1924 election produced a feeling in the markets 'nearly approaching panic' according to one director of the Bank. In a few days the sterling rate dropped 10 cents. Ironically, though, the Governor, Montagu Norman, found in the new Labour Chancellor a soul-mate. Philip Snowden (who was also to be Chancellor under the 1929 Labour Government) was a pillar of financial rectitude, being described by one historian as 'out-Gladstoning Gladstone'. Snowden, like many Labour Chancellors since, was determined that the programme of the Labour Government should not be undermined by any fears that the Party was unsound with money. Like Norman he favoured a return to the gold standard, and believed that Labour's programme could only be carried out if the markets were kept happy.

All of this meant that the Bank was moving much nearer to the centre of the political stage than it had ever been before, and that

59

in turn meant a greater level of public interest in the Bank and what it did. In the First World War, the Bank had found itself in the front line of economic policy-making. By the 1920s the level of Bank Rate had become a political hot potato: in 1925 Norman was berated by an indignant Winston Churchill, then Chancellor, for raising Bank Rate without consulting him.

In 1929 the Government was persuaded to appoint a committee to look into the provision of finance for trade and industry, the Macmillan Committee. There had been much public feeling that the City was failing to provide the capital required by British industry, preferring to send it abroad instead. (Forty years later, this feeling was to be echoed in the appointment of the Wilson Committee to examine exactly the same issue.) Clearly on the agenda was the role of the Bank of England. This worried the Bank. The mere promise of such an inquiry was enough to 'endanger our financial position both at home and abroad', according to Norman. However, on inquiring at the Treasury, he was reassured 'that the Treasury and the Chancellor will endeavour to make the reference as vague and nebulous as possible and avoid anything in the nature of an inquiry into the constitution of the Bank'. None the less the Bank made strenuous efforts to influence the composition of the Committee, even commissioning one of its Court to inquire whether possible members were 'sound or unsound' on matters of currency and credit.

There was a reason for this apparent attack of nerves: like many people, Norman was deeply conscious of the anomalies in the Bank's role – at once a key part of the state's system of economic management, yet formally a private corporation accountable only to its private shareholders. The central position of the Bank in the economy made it an obvious target for public ownership – indeed, this had been proposed several times over the previous century. It was no surprise that the manifesto of the Labour Party in the 1945 election should include the words 'the Bank of England with its financial powers must be brought under public ownership and the operations of the other banks harmonized with industrial needs'. The interesting assumption in that pledge says a lot for the attitudes of the politicians. It seems that the very secrecy with which the Bank conducted its affairs gave it an air of possessing almost magical powers.

As has already been noted, the Act nationalizing the Bank did little but change its legal status. As Hugh Dalton, the Chancellor of the time, put it, 'the Old Man of the Treasury and the Old Lady of Threadneedle Street' should be legally married 'to avoid any further danger of their living in sin'. But, beyond stating formally for the first time that the Treasury was now the master, the Act made no change to the marriage partners' various domestic duties.

That the Act did not put the Bank more firmly under political control was a tribute to the farsightedness of Montagu Norman. Throughout his time at the head of the Bank, he had emphasized the need for central banks, abroad as well as at home, to retain their independence from government. Time and again he had argued against political control over central banks: they must have, he said, formal autonomy from government and independence in their operations. Some countries have this: in the United States, for example, with its constitutional emphasis on the separation of powers, the Federal Reserve is quite independent of the US Treasury – and indeed at times appears to be following a financial policy at odds with its sponsoring government. In many other countries though, the central bank is merely an arm of government.

The constitutional relationship between Bank and government set up by the Act is studiously vague. Ultimately the Treasury is boss: as the Act says, 'the Treasury may from time to time give such directions to the Bank as, after consultation with the Governor, they think necessary in the public interest'. Such directions have never been given to the Bank. And, as a later Treasury paper provided for a Commons committee noted, the Act does not provide 'for a situation in which the Treasury might give a direction but the Bank of England might not observe it'. The reason is that by long custom the Treasury will never give directions except in 'matters of major policy in respect of which no Governor could fail to acknowledge the right of government to decide'.

The Act was aiming to put into statute law the old private and informal relationship between government and Bank without destroying its essence. The informality of the relationship, and its discretion, owed much to the sensitive matters under discussion. From the earliest days both sides have agreed on the need to keep these deliberations to themselves. Thus, writing to the Chancellor,

61

William Gladstone, in 1854, the Governor, John Hubbard, emphasized that the Bank was 'anxious to avoid any public discussion upon a proposition which they considered dangerous to public credit'. The 1946 Act enshrined such principles in statute law, and was deliberately silent on the exact workings of the Bank–Treasury axis.

Parliament has made many attempts to penetrate the wall of secrecy that surrounds this private relationship, but has had success only where the objectives have been strictly limited. The Radcliffe Committee on the working of the monetary system, which reported in 1959, recommended that the Bank improve its provision of financial statistics and information about itself. This modest suggestion was acceptable and led to a more informative annual report and to the creation of the Bank's *Quarterly Bulletin*, which features articles about the work of the Bank.

In 1968 a rather more fundamental challenge to the Bank's obscure constitutional position came from the Select Committee on Nationalized Industries. The Committee recommended that the Bank of England be regarded as just another nationalized industry and be within the remit of the Committee. In the words of the report, 'We want to see the whole picture ... what part the Chancellor plays, what part the Treasury plays, and what part the Bank itself plays.' In its inquiries the Committee had managed to extract from Sir William Armstrong, Permanent Secretary to the Treasury, this interesting, if baffling description of the independence of the Governor of the Bank: 'the Governor is not a civil servant and has had by custom a position which he has felt able to use for making public statements'. Sir William contrasted that with the position of the Chairman of the US Federal Reserve: that job entailed 'independence of action' contrasted to the Governor's 'freedom of speech'. Small wonder that the Committee was sufficiently puzzled to want to know more. The request for the Bank to be placed formally under the Committee was, however, turned down. Insiders at the Bank see this trade-off between independence and private influence as very valuable: the present Deputy Governor, George Blunden, says, 'I've been convinced with all my years at the Bank that the influence we can exert behind closed doors, in private, not through newspaper headlines, is well worth preserving, and that we probably have quite as much influence over what happens ... as do some other central banks who have got more ostensible independence.'

In 1970 the same committee looked at the 'channels of communication between Treasury and Bank'. The Committee chairman, Labour MP Ian Mikardo, complained of the Bank's reluctance to answer questions: 'As far as I can see from the evidence, every question put in this direction is met with the answer – well we have been here since 1694, so we can't be all that bad, we must know our way round the joint.' The Committee did not get answers to all its questions: the Governor, Sir Leslie O'Brien, politely declined to reveal the level of the Bank's reserves on the grounds that to do so might impair the ability of the Bank to 'do good by stealth' in its work of co-ordinating industrial and commercial rescues. The Committee concluded that 'it is in the public interest that the facts should be known about public bodies. Your committee believes that the proper interests of the Bank would in no way suffer if much of the traditional secrecy which has for so long surrounded its activities were to be dispelled.' As is so often the case with the work of parliamentary select committees, the report had little effect. Some points were conceded by the Treasury, but in essence things carried on exactly as before.

In 1979–80 the Treasury and Civil Service Committee of the Commons investigated the Bank–Treasury relationship. This committee extracted a statement from the Treasury on the division of responsibilities in the running of the money markets: 'Day-to-day operations in these markets, within the overall policy framework agreed with the Government, are very much a matter for the Bank itself, although the Treasury is kept in close touch with developments.' The Treasury went on to say that 'more important changes of direction' such as a changes in interest rate 'are discussed in advance with the Treasury and by the Governor with the Chancellor'.

Recently MPs have tried to cast light on another aspect of the private dealings between Bank and Treasury – the role of the Bank as adviser on financial and commercial matters to government. The Commons Trade and Industry Select Committee has been investigating the 1985 collapse of the tin market. (An attempt to prop up tin prices failed disastrously, with the result that tin-dealers incurred losses estimated at £165 million, and bankers losses estimated at £340 million. Several banks are now suing various governments, including that of Britain, for their failure to stand behind the markets.) The Committee has been trying to probe the role of the Bank in this. The Bank acknowledged that it had warned the Government of the impending crisis, but declined to provide confidential papers to the Committee, citing in defence the sensitivity of its relationship with government. In this case the Bank has asked to be treated as if it were part of the Civil Service – in other words, that its political masters are the ones to be questioned about what it has done. (The question of whether Parliament has the right to cross-examine civil servants has been a running argument between executive and legislature during the life of the Thatcher Government.) The Bank has argued that, just as other committees have accepted that the advice it gives ministers is confidential, so should the Trade and Industry Committee. For the moment, the battle has resulted in a victory for the Bank and the Treasury. In November 1986 the Committee conceded defeat. But that victory may prove to be just a skirmish in the long-running war: *The Times* report of the affair suggests that the Committee believes it has sufficient evidence for a 'damning report about the Bank's role in the tin crisis'. The Bank's view is simply that the Committee has not understood the difficulties it faced.

It is not surprising that Parliament has found it difficult to investigate the Bank–Treasury axis. Even insiders find it difficult to explain the relationship between what is known in-house as the 'East End' and 'West End' branches (the Bank and the Treasury). It has changed remarkably little over the years and still depends on a complex web of contacts at varying levels. And, as the financial journalist Samuel Brittan puts it, it is still a very informal process: 'more of the real business is done in conversation and less is put down on paper here than anywhere else in Whitehall'. Some groups of Bank specialists, such as the markets people, are in regular day-to-day contact with their counterparts at the Treasury, sometimes several times a day by 'phone. There are regular formal meetings between specialist branches of both institutions on technical matters; and there are sets of 'opposite numbers' meetings. Thus the Deputy Governor, George Blunden, has regular meetings or 'phone conversations with his opposite number, the Permanent Under-Secretary, Sir Peter Middleton. At the next level up the tree, the

Chancellor and the Governor meet weekly for lunch to discuss major issues of policy.

In this particular contact between Bank and Treasury there is an incidental but interesting intangible factor at work. The lunch alternates between the Treasury and the Bank. This leads to a certain quiet competition in which Claude Bonney is a key player: he is the Swiss chef to the Governor and is justifiably proud of the superb meals he produces when the two men lunch at the Bank. By contrast, rather more meagre offerings are provided by the Government's caterers. Claude would never go so far as to criticize the food available at the West End branch, but there is no doubt that the Bank likes to make a point with a subtle piece of culinary one-upmanship.

Quality of food is not the only thing to divide East and West End branches. The Bank lives a superior and very un-Civil-Service lifestyle that is on quite another plane to the dreary linoleum-clad floors and Ministry of Works desks of the Treasury. Its offices are in the grand manner – top Bank executives work in beautiful parlours, wood-panelled and filled with oil paintings and antiques, where they are waited on by uniformed servants. By contrast, Treasury civil servants have to wait their turn at the Ministry tea urn. It used to be the case that Bank pay and conditions were the envy of the Treasury: a few years ago Bank pay scales were far more generous than those at the Treasury, while the working day was a lot shorter. Today much of that has changed – Bank officials now work long hours, and the imposition of cash limits, which affect about half the Bank's operations, means that pay scales in the two institutions are much of a muchness (although the Governor is on the very non-Civil-Service rate of £90,000 a year). The ability to control the Bank's pay, at least to a limited extent, is a matter of satisfaction to the Treasury; but it may be counter-productive in the long run. Several top Bank people have recently left for very lucrative jobs in the private sector, and, if the Bank is to do its job properly, it must be able to pay market rates, certainly as far as key senior executives go.

There is also an element of the streetwise versus the intellectual that surfaces in Bank–Treasury dealing. Lord Bruce-Gardyne, a former Treasury minister, describes the Bank's attitude thus: 'They see themselves as the wise guys who know the marketplace and understand the real world and who are liable to be interfered with by a lot of hobbledehoys from the Treasury who don't understand the real world, who've a lot of absurd theories and also have chips on their shoulders. There's some truth in that.'

Hugh Gaitskell is reputed to have complained when he was Chancellor that, while the Treasury had loyalty without expertise, the Bank had expertise without loyalty. It is a clever, but not entirely accurate, remark. The Treasury now has much more expertise than it used to have in Gaitskell's day; and the Bank has found that, the closer it is to the politicians, the more it has to identify with their policies. But there is still an element of truth in the contrast. In the late 1950s, in a statement to the Radcliffe Committee, Lord Bridges, a former Permanent Secretary to the Treasury, said, 'the high officials of the Bank of England ... have long and intense training in their particular field ... officers of the Treasury are laymen'. As a result, he concluded, policy on management of the markets 'springs to a very sharp extent out of the practical experience of the Bank'. And the Bank places a higher value on expertise than on blind loyalty: as the Governor in 1969, Sir Leslie O'Brien, put it tactfully to the Select Committee on Nationalized Industries, Bank advice to government was better for being independent of the zeal which might come from civil servants who, 'living in the same departments as the Ministers who lead them, become impregnated with the Ministers' enthusiasms and aspirations'.

The very intangibility of the Treasury–Bank relationship has strengths in that it is capable of swift adaptation to changing circumstances, and allows both sides a freedom of speech that can produce better policy-making. From accounts given by insiders, discussions between the two sides are anything but a slanging match with Bank people on one side of the table drawn up for battle with the Treasury team on the other: it can often be more like a university seminar, with numerous subtle differences of view separating the various participants. George Blunden, the Deputy Governor, argues that 'we're colleagues. We are working together producing joint advice to the Chancellor. The tensions newspapers write about seem to me to appear in the headlines when I'm not aware of any tensions whatsoever. On occasions when there may have been quite a lot of disagreement then the newspapers don't get it.' Nor is advice given without thought of the political implications: 'We would be foolish not to take account of the political context. In this respect we're like civil servants ... it's no point us trying to suggest that they should do something which is utterly out of keeping with their wishes.' This is why, he believes, what he calls the 'nuclear deterrent' of the Treasury – the power under the 1946 Act to give the Bank 'directions' – has never been used.

The weakness of the informal relationship is that much depends on personalities. There is no doubt that a strong Governor can overawe a weak Chancellor and *vice versa*. Sir Stafford Cripps' boast, when Chancellor in the post-war Labour Government, that 'the Bank is my creature' is too simple. A strong-minded figure such as Lord Cromer, Governor during the 1964 Labour Government, can have an impact on Downing Street. Cromer made no secret of his distaste for the Wilson Government's policies, and said so publicly, albeit in coded Bank language. He was reputedly not unhappy that his contract as Governor was not extended at the end of his term.

Edward Heath's appointment of Gordon Richardson as Governor of the Bank of England astonished many in the City. Richardson was a former barrister who had gone on to be head of the merchant bank, Schroder Wagg. At the start of his term in office he was so low-key that the Bank was nicknamed 'the tomb of the unknown Governor'. Richardson soon changed that and in the process became, in the words of one political observer, the best Governor since Norman. He won his spurs in the secondary-banking crisis of the mid-seventies, during which his calm leadership of the Bank prevented a major financial collapse. By the time the Labour Party returned to power, Richardson had become a force to be reckoned with. Denis Healey, Chancellor under the Labour Government, describes his relationship with Richardson as one of 'creative tension'. Healey made the Governor an active part of the policy-making process: 'I used to make him argue it out in front of me with the Treasury. As often as not I took his view rather than that of the Treasury.'

Richardson's competence and authority soon put him close to the centre of politics: perhaps too close. After the Labour Government's financial crisis of 1976, which resulted in the International Monetary Fund being called on to help, it was decided by the then Prime Minister, James Callaghan, that policy on monetary matters should be made in Downing Street rather than Threadneedle Street, on the grounds that it was too important to be left to the discretion of the Bank of England. A committee of senior ministers and officials was set up to oversee monetary policy. This committee included Gordon Richardson as Governor of the Bank. Bernard Donoughue, as an adviser to Callaghan, attended that committee; he thinks it had a major impact on the Bank: 'It was dangerous in that it imposed on the innocence and virginity of the Bank of England.' Donoughue sees this episode as an important step in the diminution of the Bank's power and prestige. Once monetary policy became a key political issue, as it began to be under the 1974–9 Labour Government, the Bank was bound to be even more deeply involved in, and therefore committed to, specific policies than before. Others see this episode rather differently: Richardson's greater involvement in policy-making was, to them, a sign that the IMF did not trust a Labour government and wanted someone who believed in sound money at the heart of policy-making.

The fuss over the appointment of Gordon Richardson's successor as Governor at the end of 1982 proved that the Bank was now at the heart of politics. Numerous suitable candidates had been proposed: including Richardson's deputy, Kit McMahon, and Sir Jeremy Morse, a former Bank of England man and now chairman of Lloyd's Bank. McMahon's chances were poor: in the words of one Bank insider, he was 'less *laissez-faire* than was good for him'. Instead Mrs Thatcher chose a rank outsider, chairman of the National Westminster bank for the previous six years, Robin Leigh-Pemberton. City opinion was unimpressed. Not only was Leigh-Pemberton not a central banker; he had been a banker for just twelve years, and so was seen as lacking in experience. In a leader the *Financial Times* stated sombrely, 'the failure to choose a successor with greater experience and standing both in international and domestic banking circles is a cause for concern'. First impressions were not favourable. Within a few weeks the new Governor had managed to make some injudicious remarks about the world debt crisis and levels of interest rates.

The Labour Party's misgivings were more publicly stated. The Party was indignant that, contrary to tradition, the Government had not consulted the Opposition on the appointment, and Mr Leigh-Pemberton was also seen as a purely political appointee, teacher's pet at Threadneedle Street. Labour politicians pointed to

Mr Leigh-Pemberton's record as a Tory loyalist (he had been leader of Kent County Council). One of the Party's Treasury spokesmen denounced the new Governor as 'a crude Thatcherite monetarist', and promised that the Labour Party would remove Mr Leigh-Pemberton when it came to power. That, however, will not be easy. Bank governors are appointed for five-year terms, and there is no mechanism for removing them. Mr Leigh-Pemberton's term, which began in July 1983, will run to July 1988 – by which time the Labour Party may be in power. If it is, it will probably have to learn to live with him, thinks former Tory minister Lord Bruce-Gardyne: 'a Labour Government taking office is going to have trouble with the foreign-exchange markets or the financial markets anyway, and it would be crazy for them to go and cause greater turmoil where turmoil already exists by putting in a political appointee'. Labour spokesmen are still none too happy with Mr Leigh-Pemberton. Denis Healey says of him, 'He was not sufficiently respected in the City when he took over ... he's never really gained authority in his own constituency, and that, of course, creates a dangerous area of weakness.'

The new Governor responded to the criticism by making it clear that he would be a very different animal from his predecessors. For a start, Mr Leigh-Pemberton has been much more open in his dealings with the outside world. His predecessor refused to grant on-the-record interviews to the Press; by contrast Leigh-Pemberton is an open and relaxed man, quite at ease with journalists and happy to talk. And his managerial style is very different from the one-man-band approach of some earlier governors. Some insiders even see a deliberate change in the role of Governor, with the man at the top becoming more of an overall strategist, a sort of chairman rather than an active chief executive. This would not necessarily be a bad thing: the Bank has a reservoir of skilled senior managers perfectly capable of running it without detailed interference from on high. It seems ironic that, while City commentators have attacked other businesses for being one-man bands and not having management skills in depth, with the Bank they see the figure at the top as all important.

There has been much argument about Mr Leigh-Pemberton's toughness, for in the role of Governor it is often the man that makes the job. While Gordon Richardson made himself unpopular with the Labour Party in the wake of the IMF loan, he was scarcely more popular with the Conservatives when they took over. He was not prepared to go all the way down the monetarist road regardless of the cost to British industry; and many felt that in choosing his successor Mrs Thatcher wished to have a less strong personality at Threadneedle Street. It is this change in the relative strengths of the personalities in the Treasury–Bank relationship that worries observers such as Lord Bruce-Gardyne: he sees the dominance of Nigel Lawson, the current Chancellor, as a threat to the Bank: 'What we are witnessing at present is an extremely determined and self-confident Chancellor, who is not easily given to having his aspirations and ideas countermanded by someone else, and who has, I think, very substantially diminished the autonomy and authority of the central bank. I think it possible that his successors may regret this, because the authority and independence of the Bank is very important in exercising an influence in the City.' In fairness, many who have known Mr Leigh-Pemberton for some time feel he is a much stronger character than has been suggested: he has been variously described as 'a very clever man', 'bloody good at his job', and 'definitely not a pawn, but his own man'.

The man at the centre of all this argument is blithely unconcerned at what people say of him. He says he was surprised to be selected for the job, but adds, 'Once I'd been asked, this is probably not the sort of thing anybody ever ought to turn down, unless in their heart of hearts they simply felt they couldn't do it.' Robin Leigh-Pemberton clearly doesn't feel that. He relishes the influence and the public platform that being Governor gives him, and is outwardly confident in his dealings with government: if it comes to the crunch, a Governor has his own ultimate deterrent. 'You can push it a very long way: you mustn't and you can't constitutionally obstruct a democratically elected government; you could if necessary resign. It would be very fundamental and I think probably very damaging if it was known that the Governor of the Bank of England had been driven to resignation. It has never happened and I think both Chancellors and Governors, certainly since the nationalization of the Bank, pride themselves that we've never reached this unworthy impasse.'

Clearly Mr Leigh-Pemberton is quite happy with a role that he sees as being the overall policy-maker. He admits to not being a central banker through and through, and is content to leave much of the day-to-day business of banking to his fellow executive directors – though he has taken care in his selection of people to fill these top jobs. In George Blunden the Governor has a highly skilled deputy. Blunden, now in his sixties, has a long track record at the Bank – it was he who got the Bank's Banking Supervision Department operational. He was recalled from semi-retirement to stiffen the Bank's top-management team after the departure of the last deputy, Kit McMahon, to the Midland Bank. None the less, Mr Leigh-Pemberton has taken an active role in managing the Bank: the reorganization of the Banking Supervision Department after the Johnson Mathey Bankers debacle was very much his doing, as was the recent shake-up in the Bank's organizational structure.

The Governor is quite clearly not a typical central banker. By temperament, central bankers tend to be pessimists. From their eagle's eye view on the marketplace, they see human beings as silly, greedy and gullible, often incapable of rational action. As one wit has put it, 'an optimistic central banker is one who believes that the world is going to the dogs, but slowly'. Robin Leigh-Pemberton, by contrast, is a large cheerful man who gives the impression of enjoying life – and in particular, cricket, his private passion: 'I'm fundamentally rather an optimistic sort of person, but it would be failing in one's job if one didn't see the realistic side of life. People tend to ask for more money than they've necessarily got and it falls to the central banker to be the restraining influence.' Thus on occasions such as his Mansion House speech of autumn 1986, he is happy to deliver the dour remarks that are a part of the vocabulary of all central bankers.

Now, two years into his term, Mr Leigh-Pemberton has settled into the job. Inside the Bank he is seen as an effective team-leader, confident enough in his subordinates to let them get on with the job. The atmosphere within the Bank generally is one of relaxed competence at work. Doubts still remain: as one Bank insider put it, 'it's how the Governor handles a crisis, when one comes, that really matters. We are not sure of that yet.' The Johnson Mathey Bankers affair in October 1984, when the Bank stepped in to rescue that bank when it got into trouble, was Mr Leigh-Pemberton's baptism by fire: although his deputy at the time, Kit McMahon, handled the first crisis meetings, it was the Governor who managed things thereafter.

Over recent years, one change seems to have taken place. The Bank now looks much nearer to government. As David Scholey, a non-executive director of the Bank, puts it, 'The Bank has traditionally been in the middle ground. Now it is becoming increasingly a clearly identifiable part of the authorities, in the official structure, and less of a representative of the City.' Some see this as a new development; but one wonders if it is in reality the formal acknowledgement of what has been there all along. In an anonymous pamphlet written at the end of the eighteenth century, purporting to be the autobiography of the Old Lady of Threadneedle Street, the writer says, 'Having been twitted frequently in the course of my life with what people are pleased to term my illicit intercourse with government, it may be as well here, once for all, to admit that so far am I from being ashamed of this intercourse or considering it illicit, that I frankly avow I was affianced to the Government before I was born; in fact had it not been for the Government, had it not been understood that I was to become the accommodating friend of the Government, I verily believe, I never would have been born.'

5

The Magic of the Markets

The mystery at the heart of the Bank of England's central-banking operation, its most private and important religious practice as it were, is the management of the markets. It is an article of faith among Bank staff that outsiders, and particularly politicians, do not understand the markets and how they work. It is also the Bank's ultimate defence against political interference: when a politician proposes a course of action of which the Bank disapproves, it can be stopped with the simple statement 'it will cause problems in the markets'. This is a tactic which has been used with effect by past governors in arguments with the Treasury: Lord Bruce-Gardyne, a former Treasury minister, recalls one visit paid by the Governor to the Treasury: 'He came to say that the market was demanding a rise in interest rates ... and we argued the point at great length. But in the end the Governor was in a position to insist that he had no option. Now was that the market forcing the Governor or the Governor forcing the market? I don't know. It is certainly true that the Treasury does feel at a certain disadvantage in that sort of argument.'

The implication of the Bank's view in such situations is that markets have a force all of their own that is not susceptible to control by mere political will. The point is driven home in an appropriate form in various offices round the Bank. In the parlour of Eddie George, executive director of the bank with responsibility for the gilt-edged, money and foreign-exchange markets, is a framed quotation from the Victorian politician Richard Cobden: 'Managing the currency is just as possible as the management of the tides or the regulation of the stars or the winds.'

The Foreign Exchange Division of the Bank has a favourite quotation too, which is, if anything, even more pointed: the author this time is George Goschen, a former director of the Bank, who went on to become Chancellor of the Exchequer: 'the phrase has become usual that the foreign exchanges are "favourable" or "unfavourable", so it has been the custom to say that the foreign exchanges might be "corrected".... At all events, it must be borne in mind that which is really to be corrected is not the actual position of the exchanges, but that state of things which has brought it about.'

Those two statements sum up the Bank's attitude – an attitude that is based on a long history of attempts to manage markets on behalf of govenment. Often this has been a distasteful role for the Bank, a matter of trying to square impossible political circles. But this may be a rod the Bank has created for its own back, for it is often assumed – not least by politicians – that the power of the Bank to influence or control the market is much greater than it really is. At times it has been possible to exercise real control over the markets – as during the period of fixed exchange rates. At other times it has not: the hands-off philosophy in the foreign exchanges since 1979 is an explicit recognition of the authorities' inability to exercise control there.

During the days of the gold standard the philosophical assumption was as expressed by Goschen – that the exchange rate was merely a mechanistic reflection of other factors; and that falling gold reserves could be corrected simply by an adjustment to Bank Rate. In a statement to the US National Monetary Commission in 1909, the Bank stated that 'the Bank Rate is raised with the object of preventing gold from leaving the country, or of attracting gold to the country, and lowered when it is completely out of touch with the market rates and circumstances do not render it necessary to induce the import of gold'.

The Bank's control over interest rates generally, which has been assumed to be one of its greatest powers over the markets, took many years to come about. Before the First World War, high-street bank lending rates did not fluctuate with Bank Rate: to all intents and purposes the commercial banks used the traditional 5 per cent base rate – which dated back centuries – as the benchmark of their lending: the solid customer could expect to pay $5\frac{1}{2}$ per cent, the more speculative $6\frac{1}{2}$ per cent. As they saw it, what the Bank of England did in protecting the gold reserves was of no concern to businesses in Bradford and Birmingham. The problem in enforcing the Bank's views was the sheer size of the clearing banks: a Treasury memorandum of 1914 remarked that the Bank was 'compelled to show more deference to the wishes of the great banks ... the centre of gravity has shifted to some extent from the Bank Parlour to the Committee of the Clearing House'. Only in certain circumstances was the Bank able to enforce its views: thus, when the market was tight, getting Bank Rate to stick was no problem. On the other hand, when funds were plentiful the Bank was often unable to control rates.

The First World War and the end of the gold standard forced the Bank to be much more interventionist in the markets. The massive cost of financing the war meant that the Bank had to have more control over the markets to guarantee acceptance of the vast quantities of government paper being issued. The Bank became an active trader in the Treasury-bill market to help ensure that the financing programme could proceed steadily without disruption.

In the same way the war forced the Bank to become involved in the management of foreign exchange. The Bank's Governor set up the first arrangements for borrowing money to buy war materials in New York in 1915 (the first purchase, incidentally, was a suitably old-fashioned one, of some horses) and within two years some £400 million had been raised and spent in the United States. It was soon clear that, if the pound was not to vanish under a burden of foreign debt, the Bank would have to take an active part in supervising the market in foreign exchange. In 1915 a group called the London Exchange Committee was set up to oversee the foreign exchanges. The Governor of the Bank chaired the Committee and it had enormously wide powers of control over the markets: at certain stages of the war it met daily.

The financial turbulence of the post-war years, and the arrival of international 'hot money' (the phrase seems first to have been used in the twenties) meant that even with the advent of peace the financial markets could not be allowed to go their own way without any guidance from the authorities. Although exchange-control regulations were dismantled after the war, the state of the exchanges was a continual worry. In 1926 a Foreign Exchange Division had been set up within the Bank; and in 1929 there was official support of the sterling rate by the Bank for the first time.

The new and important role of the Bank in relation to sterling's international value was acknowledge formally by the Finance Act of 1932, which created the Exchange Equalization Account. This account was held and operated by the Bank on behalf of the Treasury: its job was described by Neville Chamberlain, then Chancellor of the Exchequer, as being 'to smooth out the variations in exchange'. The initial capital in the account was £17 million, though much more than this could be borrowed if need be. Its importance can be seen from the fact that it grew swiftly to many hundreds of millions of pounds in gold and currency. The Exchange Equalization Account still exists, and running it is one of the key functions of the Bank: it is the EEA that is being referred to when newspapers talk of Britain's foreign-exchange reserves.

Worries about the sterling exchange rate in turn fed back into the domestic economy by way of Bank Rate: the Bank of England's insistence on the paramount importance of the exchange rate meant that the interests of commerce and industry were at the mercy of fluctuations in sterling's value. It has been noted that interest rates, and thus the role of the Bank, became and have remained a central political issue, a continual source of friction between government and City. The traditional view of the Bank's role could be summed up in the famous remark of Montagu Norman that it was the job of the Chancellor to set taxes and the overall level of spending while leaving the job of fixing Bank Rate to the Governor of the Bank of England.

Not everyone saw it that way. This view of the division of responsibilities was repeatedly challenged by government. During the First World War the Treasury was continually complaining at the high level of interest rates necessitated by the Bank's insistence on protecting the exchange rate. Indeed the government, by huge issues of its own Treasury bills, even tried to influence the market by undercutting Bank Rate. On one occasion the Treasury deliberately cut its bill rate to force a cut in Bank Rate.

The Bank always found itself with a fight on its hands if it wished to raise interest rates against the wishes of government. In 1919 for example, as the economy was showing signs of overheating with a post-war boom, the Bank urged a rise in Bank Rate on the Government. The Chancellor was won over during the summer, but his Cabinet colleagues were reluctant and it was not until November that a 1 per cent rise was agreed. The Bank also won an important, albeit short-term, victory over the Treasury: it persuaded the Treasury to accept a reversion to the pre-war practice whereby the Chancellor of the Exchequer was only informed of a rise in Bank Rate an hour before it was announced. This reaffirmation of the Bank's traditional powers only lasted a few years, during most of which interest rates were falling. The moment they started rising again, ministers demanded to be consulted.

A familiar pattern was being created which has survived to the present day. Bank Rate was becoming affected by political 'stickiness'. At the insistence of the politicians, rises in the rate were too little and too late. This in turn often resulted in high rates being sustained for much longer than would otherwise have been necessary.

The increasingly intimate relationship of markets and government was further underlined in 1924. A couple of sentences in a speech by the Minister for Labour, Sir Montague Barlow, in which he referred to 'the possibility of adopting a policy of inflation as a means of financing schemes for the relief of unemployment' knocked almost 20 cents off the £–$ rate. A horrified Governor of the Bank was authorized to inform inquirers that Barlow's speech did not represent government policy.

The growing internationalism of the financial markets was another factor inhibiting the Bank's freedom to act as it wished in setting rates. From the end of the First World War no change to Bank Rate could be considered without reference to rates elsewhere, particularly in the United States. When asked by the Macmillan Committee in 1930 what influenced interest rates, Montagu Norman replied that the main factor was 'international considerations ... and so far as the international position is concerned ... we have been continuously under the harrow'. One wonders if today's Governor of the Bank would find anything to disagree with in that statement.

The pressures that all these factors placed on the Bank's market operations inevitably resulted in a growing professionalism on the part of its staff. To this day skills in market operations are highly valued within the Bank. At the same time the Bank began evolving the subtle techniques of control that have enabled it to exert a considerable influence on the operations of the markets. Discretionary powers are an important part of this. Thus, when a discount broker in 1928 complained to the Bank about conditions set by the Bank on paper he was discounting, he was treated to a firm lecture from the Governor: 'although traditionally the Bank must afford accommodation to recognized bill brokers on approved security, the *form* of accommodation and *rate* are matters to be settled on each application'. The Bank's new-found cleverness and technical proficiency paid off during the Second World War and the immediate post-war years. Once again the Bank had to raise vast sums and manage an enormously greater borrowing requirement; this was done without the problems met during the First World War, and at a reasonable cost to the taxpayer. At the same time exchange controls were smoothly introduced and remained in operation, a central part of the Bank's work, until 1979.

Today the Bank both operates in and tries to influence several different but interconnected markets. Its best-known role is in the foreign-exchange market: everyone has seen headlines such as 'Bank intervenes to support £'. In addition the Bank plays a major role in managing the various levels of the money market. This sprang initially from the Bank's position as the banker to the state, which enabled it to monitor all flows of money between the Government and the public (it is either paying out monies or receiving them on behalf of government all the time). This gives the Bank a unique overview of the money markets. At its most basic, the Bank acts on a daily basis to prevent a shortage or excess of liquidity in the market. This simply ensures that the commercial banks can meet the day-to-day demands for money made on them by their customers. The Bank's job here is a purely technical smoothing function, which happens automatically. In this very short-term market, the Bank wants its operations to be totally neutral in their impact on interest rates. But at times when the market is very short of money – for example, just after Christmas, when tax payments fall due – the Bank has to work hard to ensure that this shortage does not lead to higher interest rates.

At the next level the Bank plays its key role in influencing interest rates by meeting the needs of the discount houses, which are short-term wholesale dealers in money. (An institution with too much money in the short-term will deposit it overnight with a discount house to earn interest, while one that is temporarily short of funds will borrow from the same source.) The rate at which the Bank will buy or sell bills is an important indication of the authorities' view of the appropriate level of interest rates.

In the longer-term markets the Bank plays a major role because of the responsibility it bears for the Government's funding programme – this involves borrowing the money to plug the gap between income and expenditure, the so-called Public Sector Borrowing Requirement (PSBR). Just as in the Bank's earliest days, governments still tend to live beyond their means. (In only one year since 1952 has there been a positive PSBR – that is to say, the Government's income exceeded expenditure and there were net repayments of debt.) The excess of expenditure over income is financed by the sale of gilt-edged securities. (They are called giltedged because they are guaranteed by government.) In the past, Bank operations in this market went beyond pure fund-raising. The Bank sought to influence medium- and long-term rates by varying the yields on the gilts it sold. This led to some embarrassing incidents in which the market went on strike and refused to buy gilts because the yields, calculated to influence interest rates, were unacceptable. Nowadays that exercise has been abandoned and the Bank sells gilts at yields that enable the funding operation to continue unhindered. Attempts to influence interest rates are concentrated on the shortterm money market.

In trying to understand how these markets interconnect, and thus how the Bank has to play its cards in influencing them, a brief excursion through some economic theory is necessary. Certain key sets of economic statistics influence both the Bank's and the markets' perception of the state of the economy; and you have to understand something of the meaning and value of these statistics to understand the Bank's market operations. One of the key indicators today is a measurement of the supply of money in the economy.

The importance attached to this indicator is relatively new. In the immediate post-war years, money supply was not regarded as being of great importance by most economists and central bankers. Fixed exchange rates, exchange controls and centrally applied limits on the amount and cost of bank lending meant that the authorities could manage the economy with a degree of ease, and without needing to measure money supply: it was essentially already under official control. The central technique used was that of demand management: that is to say, the authorities tuned the level of demand – with the help of devices such as controls over hire purchase – to regulate the overall level of economic activity. Broadly, this is known as neo-Keynesianism.

This comfortable world began to fall apart at the end of the 1960s: in Britain's case the 1967 devaluation marked the turning point. The country's high internal inflation, poor productivity growth and general economic weakness made the level of its currency unsustainable relative to other currencies. It was simply not possible for the authorities to maintain its international value at the fixed level then agreed. The moral was that economic policy in one country could not be followed regardless of policy in other nations with which that country traded. The world had become too interdependent for one country to go it alone – certainly one of Britain's modest size and economic strength.

After the 1967 devaluation, the International Monetary Fund insisted on Britain imposing limits on the expansion of domestic credit. The reason was that there was coming to be seen a link between a high rate of credit expansion – money supply – and a high rate of inflation. The point was driven home by the oil crisis of 1973. This time it was not just Britain that was affected: in country after country, the massive rise in oil prices brought recession. Governments responded in traditional fashion by trying to spend their way out of recession.

The result was a burst of inflation and tremendous pressure on weaker currencies, such as the pound, in countries with the highest levels of inflation. The system of fixed exchange rates collapsed, leaving currencies to float: even the mighty dollar was forced off the gold standard and had to find its own level against other currencies. It was at this stage that policy-makers in Britain began to look seriously at the business of controlling the supply of money as a means of reducing inflationary pressures – the policy of monetarism. (Theoretical monetarism had, of course, been around for a long time.) As early as 1971 in the Bank of England's *Quarterly Bulletin*, Charles Goodhart, an adviser to the Bank, had written an article entitled 'The Importance of Money'. This article investigated the theory of monetarism and indicated that the Bank, at least, was beginning to take it seriously. But monetarism was not greeted with enthusiasm by the Treasury.

In time the new environment created by floating exchange rates convinced the Treasury to change its view. When a currency had a fixed value, which the authorities were obliged to defend, there was a form of imposed fiscal and monetary discipline on governments. If they allowed credit expansion to go mad, its effect would be felt on the exchange rate as nervous foreign holders of the currency sought to offload a depreciating asset. The arrival of floating exchange rates – which effectively adjusted the rate downwards when foreign holders of a currency sold it – removed an important constraint on irresponsible governments. A money-supply target – a central facet of monetarism – would be an effective replacement for the now non-existent control provided by fixed exchange rates.

The Treasury was therefore converted to the notion of a monetary constraint on government. It still had to convince the politicians. If there is a father of monetarism in British politics it is the then Labour Chancellor, Denis Healey. During 1976 he introduced the first targets for the growth of money in the economy. These were at first purely private and were not published. The Bank was delighted: it had been pressing the case for such targets as part of the framework of economic policy for some years. In his Mansion House speech of October 1976, Gordon Richardson made use of the Governor's traditional freedom of speech to press for open targets: 'I believe it is right to have a publicly announced monetary target.' He got his way, and an annual public target for monetary growth became a feature of the remaining Budgets of the Labour Government.

The incoming Conservative Government of 1979 took this several stages further. Mrs Thatcher decided that the growth of money supply and the level of the PSBR would be two key indicators in her economic strategy. If these were got right, it was argued, the exchange rate and the level of interest rates would sort themselves out without interference. The Tories added a further complexity to the problem of managing markets by abolishing exchange control almost immediately. This meant that anyone was free to sell sterling assets and remove his money from the country at any time. This of course had implications for the exchange rate and monetary control. It was no use imposing constraints on banks in Britain if those abroad were free to buy and sell sterling assets as they wished.

The theory behind this policy is quite simple; but in practice it has not worked out as easily and mechanically as the Conservatives hoped. In the words of one market expert, 'this government's economic policy is a bit like a Volkswagen Beetle engine; there aren't many moving parts to go wrong. But when it does go wrong, it really goes wrong.' Recently the engine has been showing signs of gasket trouble; mechanically it has not been working as it should have been. One recurring problem has been the difficulty of measuring monetary growth. The problem is that counting the money supply is a bit like doing a census of the Chinese: there's a lot of money about and it moves so fast you can't get an accurate figure. This is because it is changing its nature. There used to be two distinct kinds of money: simple money, as it were, used for transaction settlement, which was mostly kept in clearing-bank accounts; and then there was accumulated money – wealth or savings, invested in assets. As long as the two could be separately identified, monetary control – which was concerned with simple money – was not a complex task. But with modern competition for customers' funds among hundreds of financial institutions, offering such goodies as interest-bearing checking accounts, the distinction between the two, and therefore the ability to control simple money, has become blurred.

In the early days of the Government's monetarist enthusiasm, the chosen measure of money supply was sterling M3: that is to say, notes and currency in circulation and private-sector bank deposits. Broadly speaking this was simple money. The figure for sterling M3 was watched with religious devotion by government ministers – and the markets. As long as it was behaving itself this was fine; but soon it began to produce aberrations: there appeared to be no clear correlation between sterling M3 growth and inflation levels. Unable to explain why this was happening, the Treasury instead switched horses and announced in April 1982 that two other indicators were to be used as well: M1 (notes and currency in circulation and sight deposits at banks) and a thing called PSL2 – short for Private Sector Liquidity 2 – which is all the components of sterling M3, plus building-society deposits and short-dated paper with less than three months to maturity. In effect the nature of the money being measured was getting wider and wider. This also failed to perform

82

satisfactorily, and in April 1984 a further adjustment was made: the new targets were to be sterling M3, as before, and another monetary measure, M0 (notes and coins in circulation and bankers' operational balances).

This proved little more successful: yet again there appeared to be no correlation between money supply and what was happening in the real economy. The Governor of the Bank, in a speech in October 1986, hinted that the target for sterling M3 might be abandoned altogether. He argued that it was becoming more and more distorted and was painting an increasingly inaccurate portrait of the underlying growth of money supply. As one insider puts it, monetary statistics now are 'somewhat impressionistic ... a statistical fog'. Cynics suggested that this desire to abandon sterling M3 was because it was growing at almost 19 per cent as against an official target of 11–15 per cent, indicating that inflation would soon be on the way up again.

It would perhaps have been wise for befuddled politicians and civil servants to recall Goodhart's Law, named after the Bank adviser who first formulated it. This holds that any financial indicator ceases to be reliable when it is subject to official control. Regardless of whether formal targets are maintained or not, the Government and Bank are at one in insisting that monetary policy, to use the Chancellor's pet phrase, will continue 'to bear downwards on inflation'.

The other major indicator elevated to key status by the Tories is the level of the PSBR. This has also had its little local difficulties. The aim was a steady reduction in the level of the PSBR year by year: this has only been achieved by extensive sales of state assets – such as British Telecom and British Gas – which the Treasury, in defiance of normal accounting convention, insists on offsetting against the borrowing requirement, thus artificially reducing it. In real terms the amount of government borrowing is exactly the same proportion of gross domestic product as it was when the Tories took office.

Recent discussions about proposals to revise the method of recording certain key statistics – such as the PSBR, money supply and bank lending – in which the Treasury and the Bank appear to be, if not at loggerheads, certainly in disagreement, have not helped the general level of confidence of the markets. They remain convinced that it is the economic policy that is off-beam, not the statistics that are.

Which brings us back full circle to the Bank and its management of the markets. The problem is that the markets have now become accustomed to the notion of targets for money supply and the PSBR and regard with suspicion any attempt to get rid of them. The reasoning is that, if the politicans want to ditch their own figures, it must be for unsound electoral reasons. As the Governor put it recently, targets serve as 'an external discipline on the authorities, and as a guide both to the financial markets and the wider economy as to the authorities' likely behaviour'. And, if targets are of importance to the markets, then they are also important to the Bank, for what the markets think and feel is more vital than reality. In effect the Bank is trapped in a dilemma of its own making: on the one hand it wishes to control the spending urges of government by having sound monetary targets; on the other it knows that such targets are in practice not very meaningful and that money supply is very difficult to measure accurately.

This is the background against which the Bank operates in the money and foreign-exchange markets. In addition it has to walk a complex tightrope between various conflicting policy objectives. Its gilts division is in the business of selling government debt to the public – which may require high yields to ensure acceptability when borrowing requirements are high. More generally on monetary matters, it is under pressure from government to keep interest rates down: industry and homeowners are influential political groups. At the same time it must watch the sterling rate against key currencies and try and avoid precipitate changes in the rate. Too fast a fall and Britain's import bill shoots up; too fast a rise and British goods are priced out of world markets.

An example of the dilemma faced by the Bank's market managers was provided in the autumn of 1986. The collapse in oil prices, coupled with the market view of the pound as a 'petrocurrency', led to downward pressure on sterling. This was reinforced by poor trade figures in August. Faced with that, two options were available: the sterling rate could be allowed to fall, or British interest rates could be jacked up sharply to attract foreign money to the United Kingdom.

Both options were politically and economically unpleasant; so

13. Guardians of the Bank: doorkeepers John Harris and Arthur Pointer.

12. The most expensive lawn in the world: Garden Court, at the heart of the Bank.

14. The Bank's public face: the portico above the Threadneedle Street entrance.

15. *Robin Leigh-Pemberton, Governor of the Bank of England since 1983.*

16. *George Blunden, Deputy Governor of the Bank.*

17. *The Great and the Good of the City: the members of the Court of the Bank assemble in the anteroom before a Court meeting.*

18. *The Court of Directors of the Bank of England in session. They meet every Thursday morning.*

19. 9 a.m.: Ian Thompson, a Principal at the Bank, works out on the Exchequer White the country's daily requirement for money.

20. 10 a.m.: the daily money-markets meeting at which tactics for the gilts, money and foreign-exchange markets are decided.

the Bank tried to use its market skills to limit the damage. Sterling was supported expensively during the late summer and autumn, with the effect that its slide was slowed down. At the same time the Bank signalled to the markets that there was no real case for a rise in interest rates – pointing out that real British rates (that is to say, after stripping out inflation) were already almost twice those in West Germany. The line was held for a while. By the time of the Conservative Party Conference the markets were baying for a rise in rates: naturally enough the Bank did not oblige during the Conference – for which it got much City stick. (The official reason for the delay was that it preferred not to make any changes in rates till the market had settled down.) The Bank waited until 14 October before signalling a 1 per cent rise in base rates by altering its own discount rate. 'Too little, too late' stormed a *Times* editorial, and the markets promptly demanded at least another 1 per cent. The Bank did nothing, and in time the markets accepted that another rise was not coming and calmed down. As Tony Coleby, Assistant Director of the Bank's Money Markets Division, puts it, 'we have a sort of love–hate relationship with the markets ... it's always pleasing when markets which have shown signs of getting extremely nervous or excited settle down'. But he adds modestly, 'One might perhaps feel it was evidence of a degree of maturity in the markets rather than anything we've played a part in bringing about.' Similarly, when rates are under pressure to come down, the Bank also plays a waiting game: in a memorable phrase, journalist Christopher Fildes has described the Bank as 'waiting for the children to sit still before giving them their sweets'.

The actual mechanism for setting interest rates is nowadays immensely complicated. At one time, as has been noted, the Bank would simply announce what Bank Rate was to be. These days, officially the Bank is responding to market pressures, in particular the levels of bill rates. These are now seen as the key indicators of market expectation; and they could not stay out of line with the official rate for long – one must adapt to the other. At the same time, as a major dealer in the market itself, the Bank can influence both the price of money and the expectation of what the price should be. The Bank starts with a policy on rates hammered out with the Treasury; it then takes what Eddie George, Executive Director of Home Finance, terms 'an attitude' in dealings with the market. (This he defines as 'a presumption of how we will respond to certain circumstances that we anticipate'.) If the Bank is sure of its ground and thinks it can lead the way, it will succeed in making its views felt: 'We have to be very confident that the influence we are seeking to exert is credible to the market ... we can't afford to bluff; if we seek to bluff them and play with no cards in our hand then I think our credibility would be irrevocably damaged.'

At times the Bank can act credibly and put a brake on the market: in January 1986, when the markets were pushing for a 2 per cent rise in interest rates (because of worries about domestic monetary laxity), the Bank made its opposition to that clear by continuing to buy bills at a rate that reflected existing interest rates. A fall in the oil price increased the pressures for a rise in rates, which again the Bank resisted. Its view was that external factors, such as oil prices, should be reflected in the exchange rate and not in domestic interest rates. However, as this was tantamount to requesting a fall in the value of sterling, which the Bank could never be seen to be advocating publicly, nothing was said and the markets were left to work it out for themselves. In time they did so, marking sterling down and ending the pressure on interest rates. It doesn't always happen that neatly.

Like everyone involved in the markets operation at the Bank of England, Eddie George is at pains to make clear the limitations on the Bank's powers: 'We can only exert influence; we can't exert control in any of the markets.' This is in contrast to the way things were in the old days: 'When I first joined the Bank twenty-five years ago, at that stage one could simply assert an opinion; I think now we have to win an argument.'

Winning an argument with the markets is much easier if you have a lot of money to play with: and in the case of the domestic money markets the Bank does have a lot of clout; it handles thousands of millions of pounds every day. In the foreign-exchange markets it is in a much weaker position. As international trade and capital flows have increased, so has the turnover of foreign exchange round the world. London in particular now has an enormous foreign-exchange market, probably the most active in the world: a Bank survey in August 1986 estimated turnover in the London market at $90,000 million a day (this is around one third of the total daily global turnover in foreign exchange). Against this must be set the very modest level of the resources available to the Bank – at the end of October 1986 Britain's foreign-exchange reserves stood at just $21,990 million. This was after two months of effort attempting to slow down the fall of sterling: an effort that cost the reserves over $1000 million during September and October.

This is not a new position; the Bank has never had a lot of reserves to play with – in the nineteenth century the Bank often had to borrow gold from other banks to withstand pressure on the pound. And in modern times, too, the Bank has found itself going cap in hand to the International Monetary Fund or other central banks for help on a number of occasions. Despite various topping-up exercises, the most recent of which raised some $4000 million in the floating-rate note market in the autumn, the reserves are still grossly inadequate for the job the Bank has to do.

All of this means that any money spent must be used carefully and with maximum effect if the sterling rate is to be influenced. Knowing how to intervene, when to do so, and how much to spend is vital. The biggest problem is what one foreign-exchange official at the Bank calls 'the instantaneity of news'. With modern technology news, good or bad, hits every screen at once, and every dealer responds immediately. As a result the rate can sink like a stone in a matter of seconds. Take, for example, the situation on 23 October 1986. In the room of the Head Dealer of the Bank's Foreign Exchange Division three Bank officials awaited the publication of the latest trade figures. They knew that the figures were not particularly good, but felt they might be a little better than market expectations. At 11.30 a.m. a buzzer on one of the screens informed them that the trade figures had been issued. Within twenty-five seconds the sterling rate was down 30 points. The Head of the Division, Malcolm Gill, didn't panic: 'I suppose we might be considering doing a bit of something. I think at this stage not to be too overt, wouldn't you?' After some discussion, it was agreed that the Bank should act as sterling approached what is known in the trade as a 'chart point' (these are points which the markets regard much as milestones might be seen on a road – passing them is of significance). Malcolm Gill decided to do something: 'It would be a pity if we went through that too easily, without any sort of resistance. We might go a bit ... what shall we do? Ten pounds? Get one of your friends to buy ten quid and see what happens.'

'Ten quid' in Bank jargon is £10 million. It may sound a lot, but in foreign-exchange terms it is peanuts. Gill's team decided that they would provide more support at the next major chart point. At this stage Gill talked to the people whose money he was spending, the Treasury. He explained the situation and gave the Treasury an account of what had been done and what he thought might have to be done: 'I'm really just saying that I think we may need to discover during the course of the day, if this carries on, whether we should be a bit more aggressive.' In the event the Bank's small intervention had the desired effect; the market steadied and by the end of the morning the rate was only fractionally down on the previous close. But the victory was only a short-term one; within a few days, as one trader put it, 'the fundamentals had reasserted themselves', and sterling was again under pressure.

Another problem adding to the complexity is the fact that currencies now float against each other. At one time all that mattered was the £–$ rate; and Bank officials are irritated that the media still tend to concentrate on just that figure. They fix their sights on what is known as the ERI (the Effective Rate Index), the so-called basket of currencies. Each currency is trade-weighted (that is to say, its weight in the basket is determined by the amount of trade Britain does with it). This is a much more accurate – if more complex – indicator of the world value of sterling. Others have their own private key indicator: Mrs Thatcher, for example, is said to be obsessed with the sterling–Deutschmark rate.

Officially the Bank sees its role today just as Chamberlain described it in 1932 – 'to smooth out the variations in exchange'. In the old days of fixed parities it was easy: as one old hand puts it, 'When we were in the [$]2.78–2.82 rate band we always sold at 2.81¾ and always bought at 2.78¼. Simple. Now we have to worry about oil prices, other countries' interest rates, hot money and public statements by key figures.' What the Bank can't do is go against the grain of the market: if sterling is slumping, the Bank knows that, like King Canute, it can't reverse the tide. It can however have an impact at turning points: by intervening at the psychological moment of uncertainty, the Bank can massage the rate up or down. Just as in the money markets, the Bank can't bluff without having some real cards in its hands. Of course if often has information –

new money-supply or trade figures for example – that the markets don't have.

Intervention can be open or secret. Secret intervention is executed by asking a bank to buy on behalf of the Bank of England; as Malcolm Gill puts it, 'that way we can try and do a bit of good by stealth'. The other option is open market operation using brokers: 'the fact that we're in the market tends to get around because several banks will be the counter-party to our deals and that way you'll get talk in the markets that the Bank is intervening'. Trying to affect the rate by secret operation in so psychological a market would appear to be a contradiction in terms; but in such instances the Bank is often trying to improve the market position in preparation for genuine transactions on behalf of government: large sums of money are expended abroad – paying for the Army on the Rhine, for example – and this must be bought in the markets by the Bank.

And there are times when open intervention is not spotted by the market despite the wish of the Bank that it be known. That happened in autumn 1986 when the Bundesbank, West Germany's central bank, intervened in concert with the Bank to prop up the sterling–Deutschmark rate. The market was not certain that intervention was taking place and the Bank called on its smoothly competent Information Division to make sure the message got across. When financial writers made their daily calls to the press office, Bank officials were less decisive than usual in refusing to comment on possible intervention. The hint was enough for most, and soon the markets knew what had happened. No indication was given, however, of the joint nature of that intervention, as the authorities did not wish all their cards to be known; financial writers jumped to that conclusion on their own. Philip Warland, Head of the Division, sees his contacts as an important part of the Bank's market management: 'We do vary our tactics; sometimes what we say is said with more clarity. And sometimes we will tend to clam up and leave the market merely to take the evidence from the Bank's operations on a day-to-day basis. We never mislead the Press – we may not always tell them all that we know, but we will never knowingly tell them something that is untrue.'

Officially there is no policy on what sterling's effective exchange rate should be, but as one insider says enigmatically, 'Not having a policy is a way of having a policy.' The logic is that the Bank does not wish to give the markets something to aim for: in the old days of fixed rates, market speculators knew that whatever happened the Bank would defend a certain level of parity, which gave them a one-way and highly profitable bet against sterling. Now that sterling floats, the Treasury and the Bank are at pains to keep the markets guessing.

The Chancellor, Nigel Lawson, recently illustrated the perils of such a policy. In a television interview at the beginning of November 1986 he said that he 'would not wish to see sterling any lower'. Worried at the impact this might have on markets, officials hastened to point out that this did not mean there was a target for sterling which might be at, or above, its current level. Many observers think there should be one. At the end of November 1986 an independent committee of academics and businessmen, assembled by the Public Policy Centre, and chaired by a former Permanent Secretary to the Treasury, argued that there should be a publicly announced and supported exchange-rate target. International companies in Britain have supported this view, arguing that long-term business planning is impossible in a world of constantly fluctuating rates.

Others have suggested that it is time for Britain to join the European Monetary System, nicknamed the 'snake'. (This would have the effect of fixing sterling's value against European currencies.) This system was brought into operation in 1979 to reduce fluctuations among the currencies of Common Market countries – France, West Germany, Holland, Italy, Belgium, Denmark and Ireland are all members. Their currencies have fixed rates of exchange against each other – with some allowance for minor fluctuations – and the central banks of all the countries involved undertake to assist each other in protecting these rates. Britain did not participate in the system at the outset: the argument was that it was too rigid to contain sterling in its then new-found role as a petrocurrency. On top of that the strict monetary policy of the UK and the pound's special relationship with the US dollar were seen as factors making membership of the EMS unsuitable.

Today the force of many of those arguments has weakened, and opinion within the City and in industry is now strongly in favour of membership. The official line is that Britain will join 'when the time is right', but Mrs Thatcher has made it clear that she does not favour such a move for the moment. For her membership is a virility symbol: 'When we go in we will go in strong and stay in.' Although the Bank – naturally – shares the official Treasury line on the EMS, privately many Bank officials think it essential that Britain join as soon as possible. The deterioration in Britain's external trading account – partly as a result of the fast rise of imports, partly because of the decline in oil production – means, in their eyes, that sterling needs the protection of richer European nations offered by the EMS. The recent support for sterling given by the Bundesbank was seen as a hint of the benefits to come from membership.

Critics on the Continent agree that it is time for Britain to put aside isolationism and join Europe wholeheartedly. Jean-Paul Mingasson, the European Commission's Director of Monetary Affairs, has criticized Britain for its failure to join the EMS. He argued in November 1986 that staying outside had cost Britain dear: 'It has resulted in a higher level of interest rates in the UK than those that prevail in the EMS countries.' Certainly British interest rates are substantially above those prevailing in most of the rest of Europe, although whether this is entirely because the UK is outside the EMS is another question.

Certainly the most interesting comment, and one which clearly reflects private thinking inside the Bank of England, comes from the man who played such a large part in the adoption of 'practical monetarism' in Britain, Charles Goodhart. He has now moved from his job as an economic adviser at the Bank to the chair of Banking and Finance at the London School of Economics, but remains close to Bank thinking. In an article in *The Banker* in February 1986, Professor Goodhart argued that Britain should now be looking far beyond the EMS to a much more radical assimilation of its financial system with Europe's: 'I should like to move to a world in which national policy autonomy was greatly reduced, and replaced by more powerful international policy-making bodies, such as a single European central bank and a central major European fiscal authority.' This would, he argued, make it much easier for financial markets to be managed. However he concluded, with a note of regret, 'clearly this is not going to happen for a long time'. For the time being the Bank of England will just have to carry on trying to manage the tides and regulate the stars and the winds.

6

The Bankers' Banker

The Bank of England's relationship with other banks in Britain was once a very informal and private affair, rather like its relationship with the Treasury: in the latter case, as has been seen, politics put pressure on the relationship but produced few changes to its essential nature. In the case of the banks, things have changed rather more radically. Changes in the marketplace have made all banks much more competitive, and forced them to challenge the Bank of England's authority. This in turn has aroused public anxieties, which have resulted in reforms that have undermined the relaxed and unbureaucratic nature of banking supervision and given the Bank of England a statutory role in this area. The effect of this long process has been to change the status of the Bank from being the generally acknowledged first among equals to one in which it is now the formal regulator of the banking system. In short, the Bank has ceased to be at the head of a pride of lions: now it has taken on the job of lion-tamer.

It must be remembered that banks, as we would recognize them today, only emerged in late Victorian times. Up until the middle of the nineteenth century the banking system consisted of three tiers: at the bottom was the large and somewhat unstable collection of individual country banks; then there were the private London banks, which mostly concentrated on capital-raising and trade-financing; and at the top there was the Bank of England.

From its very earliest days the Bank's position as banker to the Government, and the privileged position that flowed from that, set it apart from other financial institutions and made it the bedrock of

Britain's financial system. The Bank's willingness to sort out other people's messes, on behalf of government, was an implicit acknowledgement of the responsibilities of its special position. It was to the Bank that Walpole turned to bring order out of the chaos left by the collapse of the South Sea Company in the 1720s. (This turned out to be a somewhat longer job than anyone expected: it was not until 1853 that the last annuities of the South Sea Company were redeemed or converted into government stock, thereby allowing the company to be wound up.)

When it came to dealing with a crisis, the Bank's philosophy, as noted in Chapter 2, was to leave things well alone unless the good name of the City of London or the security of the financial system was at stake. If required to act, though, the Bank could do so very quickly, as was shown with the collapse of Overend Gurney in 1866. As the Governor of the Bank at the time put it, in his report to the shareholders, 'This house exerted itself to the utmost – and exerted itself most successfully – to meet the crisis. We did not flinch from our post ... before the Chancellor of the Exchequer was perhaps out of his bed we had advanced one half of our reserves.' This money did not go to Overend Gurney, but was advanced to assist others troubled by the knock-on effects of that firm's collapse. During the various banking crises of the century, the Bank's role became formalized into that of lender of last resort to the banking system.

Such a position was never a legally defined one, nor was there any Act of Parliament giving it backing. It was a *de facto* position, springing from the simple fact that it was the Bank, and the Bank alone, that held the cash reserve to the British banking system. In the event of panic only the Bank had the resources to meet the demand for cash. It was a burden that other banks, despite being asked to, declined to share. It followed from this that whoever held the reserve for the system and was, thereby, lender of last resort clearly had considerable responsibility for, and moral authority over, the banking system. The Bank took this to mean that it should have some say in how the commercial operations of banks were managed. Typically it chose informal contact and the personal touch as the appropriate methods of control. The political economist Walter Bagehot enthusiastically endorsed this: 'In England, we can often effect, by indirect compulsion of opinion what other countries must effect by the direct compulsion of government.'

It has been noted in earlier chapters that the *laissez-faire* philosophy of the nineteenth century meant that the Bank tended to intervene as little as possible in markets and the general economy. This philosophy could not apply so easily in the case of banks. Since the operation of a sophisticated banking system depends essentially on confidence, the Bank frequently had to intervene to preserve this. The Baring Crisis of 1890 was a case in point, a classic failure of confidence in one institution; and the Bank acted speedily and decisively to ensure that the problems of one bank would not impair faith in the system as a whole. But it did not follow from this case that, whenever a bank got into trouble, the Bank would intervene. To prove the point one has only to look at the depressingly long list of Victorian bank failures – some of them on a large scale – where the Bank of England did nothing. In 1879, for example, the Bank of Glasgow suspended payment and asked the Bank of England for financial help. Assistance was refused on the grounds that there was no threat to the banking system as a whole. The fact that many customers of the bank, both individuals and firms, suffered, was neither here nor there. In that case, the Bank was probably right not to support the Bank of Glasgow and thereby ensure its continuation in business. It was clearly trading while insolvent; the manager and directors were subsequently tried and sent to prison.

In normal circumstances, when there was not a crisis, the banking system was largely left to its own devices by the Bank of England. During the period between the Baring Crisis and the First World War, the swift rise of a different type of bank – the joint-stock banks which grew out of amalgamations among the old country banks – presented a whole new range of problems. These banks did not need the Bank of England in the same way that the old private City banks did: they had enormous deposit bases, and their own branches on every major high street in Britain. At first the Bank of England was inclined to the City view that they should be ignored: successive governors refused to go to bankers' meetings. But that position became untenable as the banks' size and sheer financial muscle became evident. By the end of the First World War, the big clearing banks held 80 per cent of the country's banking deposits. Such large institutions could not be ignored. By then the Bank was attending regular meetings with the clearing banks every quarter.

94

The sheer size of these new banks was, however, beginning to cause political ripples: a wave of amalgamations and takeovers had resulted in just five major clearing banks dominating the high street by 1918; and there was public concern at the possible emergence of a monopolistic 'money trust' operating against the public interest. Since the Bank declined to take a clear stance on the matter, a committee of inquiry was appointed by the Chancellor of the Exchequer, Bonar Law, to consider the implications. After much discussion – going so far as the drafting of a Bill, later withdrawn, to outlaw further amalgamations – it was agreed to draw up a list of which banks might amalgamate with which. As the rules were somewhat complex, interpretation of them was handed over to the Governor of the Bank. This was the first in a series of cases in which public disquiet about the banking system led, via the threat of legislative action, to a private agreement to leave the problem to the Bank. In this case the Bank's arm had to be twisted by government before it would take on this new responsibility.

The effectiveness of the Governor's authority over the banking system was soon called into question. In 1925 Barclays Bank began forming several overseas banks already under its control into a separate operating subsidiary to be called Barclays (Dominion, Colonial and Overseas). This would be 'A British Empire bank under the Barclays flag' explained a proud chairman. The Bank of England was not convinced: it saw the new creation as a dangerous potential addition to Barclays' liabilities which, if it went wrong, might threaten the survival of the parent bank. This was not an idle fear: two of the three banks involved in the amalgamation were in a shaky condition. In a letter to the Chancellor outlining its opposition, the Bank expressed fears that 'conditions [overseas] may differ widely from those at home and . . . local interests may at times conflict with those of this country'. Barclays ignored these views, and the Bank retaliated by using what powers it had: Montagu Norman refused to open an account for Barclays DCO at the Bank and announced that the new bank would not be 'approved' for discounting at the Bank. This had no effect and Barclays went ahead with its plans, effectively ignoring Norman's wishes.

However, it could be said that the Bank has had the last laugh – although it took sixty years for Norman's warning to be borne out. Barclays' disposal of its South African interests in the autumn of

1986 – at a rather modest price – seems to suggest that the Bank's remarks about differing conditions prevailing in other countries had some force in them.

The Bank's worries about British banks' involving themselves in potential liabilities abroad were borne out in September 1931, when it was approached for help by the Anglo-South American Bank. This bank was involved extensively in financing the then-flourishing British trade with Latin America. In particular it had made large advances to the nitrate business in Chile, which had hit problems in the late twenties with falling prices and the arrival of cheaper artificial substitutes. Given the large role Anglo-South American played in Latin American trade, and the amount of its paper held by the discount market, the Bank of England had no option but to help. £1 million was advanced at once; and it soon became clear that much more would be needed. A worried Governor felt forced to approach Whitehall for help, and eventually a Treasury guarantee was given, underwriting the Bank's support operation. Despite putting its own nominee into the chairman's seat at Anglo-South American, the Bank felt the only solution was a takeover. Eventually it persuaded the Bank of London and South America, part-owned by Lloyds, to do the decent thing. In this case, the Bank's actions did not conform to its own unwritten rule of never saving people from the consequences of their own folly. By acting to support British trade and the London discount market, the Bank had in effect also saved the shareholders of Anglo-South American.

A problem of a different nature emerged during 1928, with a crisis involving one of the smaller clearing banks, Williams Deacons. Based in Manchester, Williams Deacons had considerable loans outstanding to the depressed industries of the region. Many of these were non-performing, and it was clear that, unless quick action was taken, a clearing bank would fail for the first time. The Bank was called in and in turn asked its auditors, Deloittes, to look at the problem. A statement of affairs was prepared, and the Bank undertook to guarantee some of Williams Deacons' advances in order to keep the bank open. Meanwhile a team from Deloittes remained at the bank as watchdogs. The operation was a highly secret one, the purpose being to maintain public confidence that all was well at Williams Deacons.

Clearly the only possible long-term solution was to find a buyer for the bank. Eventually the Royal Bank of Scotland was persuaded to take over the ailing clearer, but only after the Bank of England had given a juicy inducement by offering to transfer the business and premises of its own West End branch in Burlington Gardens to the Royal Bank. (This action also suited Norman's book for another reason – he was keen for the Bank of England to get out of anything that smacked of competitive commercial banking.) In the event, even this was not enough: the Royal discovered that the state of affairs at Williams Deacons was worse than expected, and the Bank of England had to stump up further large sums of money after the takeover. The eventual bill was some £3.2 million.

It was not just clearing banks that found themselves in trouble in those difficult times. In July 1931 Lazards merchant bank asked for help. In this case the problem was misbehaviour in the Brussels office, which had cost the firm £6 million. The Bank decided to help because the failure of Lazards 'would probably give rise to a state of panic in the City and create serious difficulties for other important houses', as the Committee of Treasury put it. Lazards' status as a member of the Accepting Houses Committee, the elite of London banks, was the key: under no circumstances would the Bank allow one of these banks to go under. The reputation of the London market depended on their survival.

Lazards was by no means the only accepting house to require support; and it was inevitable that the Bank should demand some *quid pro quo* for its help. The first informal aspects of banking supervision proper grew out of this: from 1929 the Bank expected each accepting house to keep the Governor informed of its capital position. In 1937 one house objected to this prying; a threat from the Bank to refuse the firm's paper quickly produced a change of heart. Because the Bank's ultimate sanction – that of refusing acceptances – lay with the Discount Office, it was this department of the Bank that evolved as the main supervisory arm. In the 1920s the Bank had instituted a regular meeting every Thursday afternoon between the Governor (or Deputy Governor) and the principal discount houses; at this highly informal and private session many confidences about the banking system were exchanged. There was no question about the Bank's authority here: without the approval of the Bank no discount house could trade.

With the clearing banks there was no such power: they had to be cajoled into doing what the Bank wanted. The long battle to persuade the clearers of the desirability of publishing meaningful financial statements was a case in point. In 1921 Norman was pressing for them to be produced; but it was not until after the Second World War, in 1946, that the clearing banks agreed to the publication of statements of position that made sense. Similarly, Norman's experience of industrial rescue work, discussed more fully in the following chapter, suggested to him that the clearing banks were not doing all they might to support British industry. Repeated representations led to long discussions of the problem, but little else. Again, it was not until after the war that the clearers were persuaded formally to take a more supportive role in British industry by their shareholdings in the Industrial and Commercial Finance Corporation and the Finance Corporation for Industry, but both were clearly Bank of England rather than clearing-bank initiatives.

Despite such occasional tiffs, the generally clubby atmosphere of the banking business continued happily into the post-war years. As one Governor of the Bank put it in 1957, 'If I want to talk to the representatives of the British banks, or indeed of the whole financial community, we can usually get together in one room in about half an hour.' The story of post-war banking regulation is the story of the gradual breakdown of that cosy club under pressure from the outside world.

The issuing of 'requests' illustrates the point. The 1946 Act nationalizing the Bank allowed it to give 'directions' to commercial banks on certain matters (notably areas such as credit control). The Bank declined to give directions, preferring instead to issue 'requests'. At the end of the Second World War, the Bank only needed to issue such 'requests' to a handful of institutions to convey its views on lending; by the end of the sixties, the 'requests' were going out to more than 260 institutions. Faced with such numbers, the Bank tried to exercise its powers indirectly, and accordingly put pressure on the various different types of financial institution to form trade associations through which its views could be made known.

The level of liquidity of banks and the control of the amount of credit in the banking system were – and still are – vital concerns of the Bank of England. The Bank would issue 'requests' for certain levels of liquidity to be maintained – usually 8 per cent to be held in cash and 28 per cent to be held in relatively liquid form. Bank

Rate was clearly the key weapon in the control of credit, but another was created in the post-war years. At times when the Treasury wanted to tighten credit, the banks would be asked to place 'special deposits' at the Bank of England, a sum over and above their normal level of deposits. This had the desired effect of making credit harder to obtain. At other times banks would be requested to show bias in their lending in favour of certain categories: exporters, for example.

Consumer and political pressure eventually removed these techniques of market control. In May 1967 the National Board for Prices and Incomes, a government body, produced a report on bank charges which was a bombshell. It argued that the set of restrictive practices then in operation in the banking sector – effectively a cartel arrangement whereby all banks offered a similar service at a similar price with no competition – was against the public interest. It demanded sweeping changes to make the banking system more responsive to the market. This was followed by a Monopolies Commission report which was highly critical of the 'soporific effect' of such restrictive practices on banking. These reports led to a wave of public and political demands for more competition among banks.

The Bank responded in May 1971 by producing a document entitled 'Competition and Credit Control', which became the basis of a new policy that took the same name. The object was, as the Governor put it, 'to permit the price mechanism to function efficiently in the allocation of credit, and to free the banks from the rigidities and restraints which have for too long inhibited them'. Many of the limitations on lending discussed above were abolished – all the jargon of 'ceilings', 'qualitative' and 'quantitative' controls vanished. The banks' interest-rate cartel was also dismantled and they were encouraged to compete more actively for business. Two weapons were retained: special deposits and Bank Rate.

But the new-found emphasis on markets changed the nature of both of these. In October 1972 Bank Rate became MLR, short for Minimum Lending Rate. The idea was that, instead of being imposed by the authorities without reference to the marketplace, MLR would reflect what was happening in the market: specifically the level of interest set by the weekly tender for Treasury bills. It was, however, a somewhat cosmetic change: the Bank's influence in the Treasury-bill market was such that its views on what the correct level of rates should be was bound to carry considerable force. Special deposits also changed their nature: different factors were now included in the calculation of a bank's reserves, and what had been a sharp weapon of control became somewhat fuzzy in actual operation.

Competition and Credit Control (CCC) was a political triumph for the Bank. For years since the war the Bank had been obliged to do the dirty work of Whitehall in trying to force the economy, via the banking system, to do what the politicians wanted. The criticism of the banking system for being uncompetitive was an ideal chance to escape from Whitehall's clutches. The Bank was only too happy to get back to the old system of leaving the market to make up its own mind as to priorities. Although the CCC policy was stimulated by political pressures, it was, as one Treasury official put it, '70 per cent the Bank, 25 per cent the Treasury and 5 per cent the politicians'. It was the Bank's good fortune that the chance to enact CCC should have come during the period in office of a government committed to reducing the state's role in the economy.

All these changes happened as the banks were facing a real challenge for deposits from other financial institutions in the marketplace. The building societies, for example, had increased their share of domestic deposits substantially during the 1960s: by 1970 they held almost 29 per cent, as against 32 per cent for the clearing banks. The banks responded by offering new facilities to depositors or would-be depositors; credit cards, personal loans and other ideas were introduced to stimulate customer loyalty. In 1968 Barclays even created what would have been unheard of a few years before – a marketing division. At the same time new financial markets were springing up – the so-called secondary markets – where new forms of financial instrument, such as inter-company debt, local-authority loans, and interbank loans were the currency. And new wholesale money markets, many of them in foreign currencies, were springing up in London. British banks hastened to take a major role in all of these.

In all of this the traditional branch networks of British banks were coming to play a less significant role as providers of funds to the banking network. Between 1962 and 1972 deposits in the London interbank market rose tenfold. This wholesale money became an important part of bank funding. That created a problem: unlike customers' deposits, which were, if not free, certainly very cheap, wholesale money had to be paid for. That meant it had to earn a good return. Banks searched for the best returns and found that all too often the property sector provided them. In part this was the fault of the Labour Government, which in 1964 introduced a ban on office developments in London and shortly afterwards resrictions on development in the rest of the South East. The effect of this was to guarantee spectacular returns for anyone owning existing property in this area; between 1965 and 1970 office rents in the City went up fourfold.

By the time the CCC policy arrived there was a pent-up demand from the banks to invest in property. Previously Bank of England controls had limited loans to this sector. With controls removed, the banks went on an orgy of lending to property companies: in just two years from the end of 1971 this increased 400 per cent, while lending to industry rose in the same time by less than 50 per cent. The inevitable result was a massive rise in the prices of commercial property in particular. The more prices rose, the happier the banks were to lend. The head of one property company remarked that if he had gone to his bank with a proposal to build a skyscraper on the Old Man of Hoy (a massive rocky outcrop in the Orkney Islands), 'they'd have given me the money twice over'.

The Bank of England expressed its worries at the large scale of clearing-bank commitment to the property sector; but in vain. The clearers' response was to lend even more, but indirectly via the network of secondary or fringe banks that had grown up. Thus a property-developer who had reached the limits of his overdraft with a clearer was told to apply round the corner at a fringe bank where the same money – deposited by the clearer – would be available, though at a higher price. These fringe banks, known as '123 banks' after the section in the 1967 Companies Act that authorized the Board of Trade to license them, had sprung up in large numbers to meet banking needs not being met by the clearers.

In summer 1973 the authorities began to take control of the situation again: interest rates were abruptly removed from market control and raised in the traditional way. At the same time the so-called 'corset' was introduced, a control on the amount of bank borrowing in the money markets. It was not until late in the autumn that these measures began to take effect, and then with results that were almost catastrophic to the banking system.

Most people date the beginning of the secondary-banking crisis to November 1973. At the end of that month it was revealed publicly that the fringe bank London and County Securities was in trouble and that it had been rescued by a consortium headed by the First National Finance Corporation, the biggest of the secondary banks. The Bank of England did not take a part in this, arguing that fringe banks were not its responsibility. Within a month that view changed as it became clear that a substantial number of fringe banks were in trouble, and, if they were in trouble, so too were a number of clearers who had substantial deposits with them. The collapse of Cedar Holdings on 20 December 1973 forced the Bank into action. After a meeting the next day with the chairmen of the major clearers, the new Governor, Gordon Richardson, announced that the Bank and the clearers between them would put funds into fringe banks in trouble.

This was the beginning of the famous 'lifeboat', known more formally as the Control Committee. Chaired by the Deputy Governor and with a member from each of the clearing banks, the Control Committee aimed to recycle clearers' deposits withdrawn from fringe banks that were apparently sound so as to help those in trouble. The hope was that a declaration of support from the Bank of England and the clearers would be sufficient to stop the loss of confidence in what were believed to be fundamentally sound businesses. It was soon clear that this was not to be and that the size of the problem was much larger than at first thought.

Within three months the lifeboat had doled out more than £400 million and the figure was rising rapidly. By the end of 1974 the amount committed was nudging the limit of £1200 million which the clearers had placed on their contributions. Initially they had agreed to provide 90 per cent of the money, with the Bank putting up the balance. As the clearers refused to put up any more cash, the Bank had to increase its contributions, and the lifeboat's support reached its peak figure of £1285 million in March 1975. The problem was that the property sector, to whom the fringe banks had lent much of their money, was in crisis: major property firms were going bust each week, and parallel to the Bank's lifeboat operation for the banks was a property salvage operation run by Kenneth Cork, senior partner of the City insolvency firm Cork Gully.

The strain on the clearers' balance sheets was immense: at the height of the operation 40 per cent of their reserves and deposits were committed to the work of the Control Committee. The atmosphere of crisis was such that the solvency of some of the best-known institutions in Britain was being called into question. There were strong rumours around the City that one of the clearers was in trouble, and in November 1974 the chairman of the National Westminster Bank was forced to issue a public statement to the effect that his bank was under no liquidity pressure whatsoever.

The rescue process was by no means a simple one, and the members of the Committee had numerous wrangles about who should be rescued. The clearers, anxious to limit what appeared to be an open-ended commitment, called on the Bank to draw up a list of banks that would be supported come what may. The Bank refused, pointing out that such a list would effectively condemn those not on it to certain death. Furthermore, the notion of separating the deserving and the undeserving was not as simple as it sounded. The classic problem facing the Committee was that of distinguishing between institutions that had a crisis of liquidity – that is to say, a temporary shortage of cash – and those that were hopelessly insolvent. At the moment of crisis it was not always easy to tell the difference. The Bank preferred to deal with cases as they arose on an *ad hoc* basis. Bank officials later admitted that this allowed some doubtful characters to be saved who should have been allowed to go to the wall; even so, some fringe banks were not rescued.

In one case, in October 1975, the Bank organized a rescue at its own cost – for the very traditional reason that this particular collapse would threaten the financial reputation of the City of London. Slater Walker Securities was very much a fringe bank, but, because it was authorized to deal in foreign exchange and had a position in the Eurocurrency markets, the Bank determined to rescue it. This cost the Bank dear: although an exact figure has never been revealed, an independent accountant's report into Slater Walker calculated that the Bank had given guarantees of £70 million and indemnities of another £40 million.

The Control Committee is still in existence, although the last 'client' has now repaid its borrowings – some recovery is still expected from outstanding liquidations. On balance, because of the high price charged by the Committee members for their support, it is probable that the banks backing the lifeboat came out at least all square and more probably ahead of the game.

The immediate crisis over, thoughts turned to the lessons. One thing was immediately clear: the slap-happy system of regulation that had existed before the crash had to go. Critics noted that the term 'bank' seemed very easy for a business to acquire – there were seven different statutes under which you could tack the word on to your business. The famous section 123 of the Companies Act was an immediate target: the implication of an 'authorized institution' was that it was run in a proper manner and subject to regulation. This was far from the case. The Department of Trade had given only cursory inspection to companies before granting them 123 status; and the Bank of England, although some of the banks under its control were section 123 banks, had exercised little supervision. The sheer laxity of the wording of the Act had allowed too many irresponsible people to set themselves up in business as banks: the fuzzy division of authority between the Bank and Whitehall had created a gap for them to enter the market unobserved.

Inevitably the Bank's regulatory mechanism came under attack. It was not a very impressive organization, consisting as it did of some fifteen staff working in the Discount Office. They were well informed enough about the affairs of discount houses, with whom the Office dealt, but their knowledge of the wider world of financial institutions was dismal. (Clearing-bank supervision was run through the office of the Chief Cashier.) The supervisors tended to rely too much on trust and membership of the City club in their judgements: as the Principal of the Discount Office put it in his explanation for the failure of the Office to vet 123 banks more thoroughly, 'I think we took those on trust ... the basis being, of course, that if you ever found a chap out in a lie, he was finished for ever. You assumed nobody would be so stupid.'

Having been found so wanting in time of crisis, the Bank proceeded to put its own house in order with commendable speed. In July 1974 a Banking Supervision Department was created inside the Bank, under the control of George Blunden, now the Deputy Governor. It had twice the staff of the old office; and this figure grew to seventy within three years. The new division dramatically increased its demands for information from the banks, in particular concentrating its efforts on the 123 banks, control of which it effectively took away from the Board of Trade. Key banking ratios were subjected to much more detailed examination than ever before. But the Bank also recognized that the problem of supervision was no longer a matter that could be dealt with within national frontiers: in 1974 at a meeting of the Bank for International Settlements (the international bankers' club) in Basle, the Bank took the lead in persuading other central banks of the principle of 'parental responsibility'. This means that any branch of a bank that gets into trouble is regarded as being primarily the responsibility of its parent bank, wherever that is based. This was followed by requests to parents of banks operating in London for what are known, in quaint banking parlance, as 'letters of comfort' – that is, formal undertakings to support the branch or subsidiary in time of crisis, should such support be needed.

Despite this flurry of activity, the politicians had decided that the business of banking regulation required some statutory spine to it to prevent such crises from happening in the future. The result was the 1979 Banking Act. This insisted that anyone taking deposits from the public must have a licence to do so, and created two levels of bank – the 'recognized bank' (the first division, as it were) and the 'licensed deposit-taker' (the second-division bank). An important emphasis in the legislation was consumer protection. A Deposit Protection Fund was created to which every bank had to contribute and from which depositors in failed banks could claim a certain amount of compensation (though this was limited to 75 per cent of sums up to £10,000). The Bank was not happy with this provision: it seemed to it almost an encouragement to people to leave their money with sharp operators. But the Bank scored a major victory with this Act: henceforth all banking supervision was to be confined to the Bank of England. This was a snub to those forces in Whitehall which wanted supervision to come under a government department.

In operating the 1979 Act the Bank retained many of the informal techniques of the old days: the principles to decide whether an institution was a full bank or not were subtle in the extreme. To be in the first division a bank had to have 'a high reputation and standing in the financial community. ... in forming its judgement ... the Bank has regard to market opinion and takes soundings among other institutions as appropriate', according to the Bank's own manual of supervision. The quality of the management was a consideration, as was evidence that business would be conducted 'with integrity, prudence and appropriate professional skills'. One-man businesses were not wanted: under the so-called 'four eyes' provision, any bank had to have at least two individuals at the top directing the business.

Banking Supervision is now one of the largest divisions in the Bank, and employs 150 people, watching over some 600 financial institutions. It is also one of the few departments of the Bank to make use of outsiders – secondees from other banks or accountancy firms who join it for a two-year stint. This a rare recognition by the Bank that it does not have all the skills needed for the job in-house. But the secondees have been surprisingly impressed by their time inside the Bank: one, from Barclays, found his Bank colleagues 'really rather unassuming, very conscious of their few failures and almost dismissive of their many successes'. The atmosphere he described as 'collegiate rather than hierarchical', with considerable emphasis on informal discussion. That extended to supervisory visits as well: he noted that, of the sixty such visits he made, only one involved a formal invoking of the 1979 Act – all the others were by mutual agreement.

The system is heavily dependent on informal discussions with banks: these are, as one Bank official puts it, 'the cornerstone of the system of supervision'. These discussions are built around half-yearly 'prudential visits' at which a team from the Bank, having studied a particular institution's accounts and returns under the Banking Act, discusses any issues arising at a lengthy meeting with the bank's senior management. 'The supervisor's job is about judgement, it's about making your mind up whether the management of an insti-tution is up to the job', says Brian Quinn, a shrewd Scot who is Assistant Director of Banking Supervision. 'There's a lot of give and take at these meetings. It isn't our job to stop them doing business but to help them do it prudently. We want to see that there are systems in place to monitor risk.'

Quinn sees the Bank's job as persuading people to stop and think: 'When animal spirits in the City are running high ... I think there's a role for the supervisor, just to ask them to hesitate, just put in a peg, just to stop them running too fast.' Formal sanctions, first provided under the 1979 Act, have rarely been imposed on major banks, although between 1979 and 1986 some two dozen licensed deposit-takers had their licences withdrawn. The Bank prefers persuasion: as Brian Quinn puts it, 'Much the greater part of our work is trying to persuade institutions, when they need persuading, that they should think again about the way in which they're conducting the business.'

Critics of the system argued that it was far too informal and not dependent enough on banks' being required to meet formal ratios limiting risk and the like. The Bank insisted that such bureaucratic procedures were unnecessary and ineffective. A further scandal in the secondary-banking area has forced the Bank to think again.

On Sunday 30 September 1984 some 200 City bankers had their weekends ruined by an urgent summons to a meeting at the Bank of England. When they arrived they were informed that there were only hours left in which to save Johnson Mathey Bankers (JMB), a subsidiary of one of the world's leading gold-bullion dealers. The bank was in serious financial trouble, and if it was to open on Monday morning it needed new financial backing urgently. After hours of discussion and negotiation, continuing through the night and sustained by coffee and sandwiches, a £250-million rescue package was put together and signed at 8.30 on Monday morning, just in time to enable JMB to open its doors for business. Under the terms of this package the Bank of England became the owner of the ailing bank.

The collapse did not come as a complete surprise to all. For weeks before there had been rumours that a bank was in trouble, and during the preceding week dealers in the far East had refused to accept JMB's paper. The Bank of England had known somewhat longer that all was not well. What it did or did not do during that time became a crucial issue in the argument over banking regulation and its future.

JMB had been set up by the London bullion dealers Johnson Mathey as a bank specializing in financing Third World trade. The new subsidiary prospered, and its loan book increased ninefold between 1980 and 1984. Just before the crisis it stood at £405 million. The problem was that some of these loans, including some very large ones, were effectively non-performing by the summer of 1984. However, these were not picked up by the bank's auditors, Arthur Young McClelland Moore: in June 1984 the firm signed JMB's accounts without adding any form of qualification. The Bank of England's supervisors were not so happy, and asked the auditors to look again. The second search revealed the existence of these highly suspect loans. One interesting question is why the Bank did not then act at once to stop JMB trading. George Blunden, the Bank's Deputy Governor, says that would have made little difference: 'We might have got onto it a month or two earlier, but it would still have been a case of insolvency. What had happened there was that quite suddenly, almost unbelievably, the management had gone in for an enormous amount of very foolish lending ... if we'd got onto it a month earlier there might not have been quite such a mess for us to clear up, but there would still have been a mess.' Today the view of some in the Bank is that if they had known the extent of JMB's problems – that it was not just short of cash but effectively bust – the rescue would never have been mounted. But that is an opinion based on the wisdom of hindsight.

At the time the Bank had no hesitation in acting: the problems at JMB were serious enough to drag down its parent, and that could have disastrous effects on the London bullion market. Aside from that, as George Blunden puts it, there was always the risk of 'a spread of infection through the banking system'. The decision to act presented the Bank with a further difficulty – for the 200 bankers it had summoned to the Sunday meeting were reluctant to pick up an as-yet unquantified tab that could run into millions. At the meeting the Bank had been forced to provide some of the indemnity package raised to cover JMB's possible loan-book losses. Although none of the package was actual cash, it was a potential call on the Bank's reserves. Nor was this all: a few weeks later, as the extent of JMB's illiquidity became apparent, the Bank was forced to 'deposit' £100 million with its new subsidiary to stop it going bust. £75 million of this was later converted into capital and £25 million into loan stock.

It is a moot point whether the Chancellor of the Exchequer, Nigel Lawson, knew, or approved, of this use of what was, if not taxpayers' money, then certainly public funds, in that they belonged to the Bank and therefore the nation. The Bank argued that it was only doing what Parliament had suggested it do: namely, use its own funds to back such rescue operations. The Bank, somewhat ingenuously, affected to regard this deposit of £100 million as a normal commercial transaction between a parent and a subsidiary –

a viewpoint that was not found very plausible by Parliament. The row over the handling of JMB erupted into some of the worst-tempered scenes witnessed at Westminster for some years, with the Labour MP Brian Sedgemore even describing Nigel Lawson as a 'snivelling little git'. More seriously, widespread concern was expressed as to how the intervention had come about and why the Bank of England appeared to be acting entirely on its own initiative. Mr Lawson, clearly furious at the way the Bank had handled matters, responded by appointing a committee to look into the implications of the affair for banking supervision. Despite his anger he was determined that the affair should be dealt with in-house. This was reflected in his choice of members of the committee: all bar one were Treasury or Bank of England appointees, and the chairman was the Governor, Robin Leigh-Pemberton.

At the same time the Bank conducted its own internal inquiry into what had gone wrong. It concluded that the Banking Supervision Department needed to be strengthened by the addition of more qualified staff. The Bank also looked at the role of the auditors. (This was hardly surprising given that the Bank had decided to sue Arthur Young McClelland Moore for £200 million over its part in the JMB affair.) The Bank suggested that it wanted a closer relationship with auditors, one that would not be confined to the annual audit. Although emphasizing that it did not want auditors to act as 'whistleblowers', the Bank's proposal caused protest in the accountancy profession, many of whom wondered what would happen to their traditional and confidential relationship with their clients. (As an interesting sidelight on this, a recent study of corporate fraud concluded that more information about fiddles came from wronged mistresses getting revenge than from auditors – which would suggest either that not many auditors have been keeping their eyes open, or that shareholders and regulators alike should welcome board-members' taking on mistresses!)

Most of what remained at JMB was disposed of by the Bank in April 1986. No one is yet sure what the final bill will be: the Bank's own estimate of its maximum potential liability is £21 million, and in practice it could be a lot less. If that is so, the bill will be much smaller than many of the Bank's critics in Parliament feared. But there will be another price to pay. As a result of the JMB affair, the Government has introduced a new Banking Bill which will tie the hands of the banking community – and the Bank of England's supervisory department – more tightly. The new Bill could be seen as a somewhat public slap in the face for the Bank's regulators. It provides for a Board of Banking Supervision, outside the Bank's control and backed by statute, to advise the Bank. If the Bank does not wish to accept the Board's advice, it must inform the Chancellor of its reasons. For some observers the Board of Banking Supervision has all the makings of a potentially powerful government quango, which could in time supplant the Bank's authority in this area. Other provisions abolish the distinction between 'recognized banks' and 'licensed deposit-takers', setting out just one definition of a bank; require any enterprise seeking banking status to have a paid-up capital of at least £5 million; and oblige financial institutions to notify the Bank of any individual loan or exposure which exceeds 10 per cent of their capital base. A number of clauses markedly increase the Bank's powers: it can demand more information from banks, and has the right to block the purchase of controlling share-holdings in UK banks. And auditors are released from their duty of confidentiality to clients if required to pass information to the Bank about those clients.

Bankers are not exactly happy about these swingeing new powers: in November 1986 the British Bankers Association considered the clause limiting the amount of exposure to one customer 'to be unnecessary and to mark a step in the wrong direction'. The Bank of England sees the new Bill as confirming its position as the key regulator of the British banking structure; but, as banking supervision becomes more hedged about by statutory rules, tension must inevitably arise between the new legal rigour and the old informal flexibility so loved by the Bank. And behind it all stands the new Board of Banking Supervision, which could well represent Whitehall's Trojan horse in the private world of banking. As Lord Seebohm, a director of Barclays Bank, lamented in the House of Lords during the debate on the 1979 Banking Act, 'If we go on chipping away at the flexibility and the old customs of the City ... we shall sooner or later find that the City loses its paramount position as the financial centre of the world.'

7

A Nod and a Wink

In the area of banking supervision, as has been noted, the Bank of England has been given a formal and legal role, one laid upon it by Parliament. But over the years the Bank has just as happily taken a role in the management of affairs in places where it has no licence, let alone statutory powers, for its operations. In these areas it has relied on its considerable authority and contacts to take a major role. Sometimes the Bank has involved itself following a request for it to intervene; at other times it has thrust itself to the forefront of a situation in defence of the good name of the City. Where it has some kind of authority behind it, it tends, as one insider puts it, 'to leave the cane in the school cupboard, but never let anyone forget it's there'. In other cases it must rely on what is known in the City as 'a nod and a wink' – a highly informal and personalized type of authority that, as another Bank man puts it, relies on 'persuasion bereft of any sanction'. Wrongdoers have to be persuaded that it is in the interests of all to toe the line. Some of these areas of activity are highly traditional – such as the Bank's long-standing general oversight of City markets – but many others are outside its usual sphere of operation.

One of the least known of these, though it is an area that the Bank has been involved in for many years, is the management of industrial rescues. The Bank has always felt that it has a clear duty to support the financial system in times of crisis. It has come to develop the same feeling towards the industrial sector. Its role in this area is, in a sense, a legacy of its days as a private and competitive commercial banker. As far back as 1815, the Bank found itself involved in helping a Newcastle ironworks through a sticky patch. The company in question was associated with another firm that banked with the Bank of England. Most of these early rescues tended to involve firms that had accounts at Bank branches: in 1835 £9000 was advanced to assist the Wolverhampton firm of Thorneycroft, which banked at the Birmingham branch. Sometimes such attempts to help went wrong: in 1848 the Bank found itself the proud owner of a copper works near Swansea that had gone down after being advanced money. Four years later the Bank was still desperately trying to find a buyer for the business, 'whether at a profit or at a loss'.

The troubled conditions of the years between the two world wars pushed the Bank heavily into the business of supporting industry. It was not a planned intervention, but, like many other things the Bank has done, it just happened. The first case involved a client of the Bank's Newcastle branch, the armaments company Armstrong Whitworth. At the end of the war, encouraged by the promise of a large overdraft from the Bank, Armstrong had expanded its business somewhat rashly. Within a short space of time heavy competition and the resulting pressure on margins had the firm in trouble. The Bank was obliged to put up some more of its own money and introduce a company doctor to get things right. The Bank also found itself forced into restructuring the business and selling off chunks of it. Even so, it was not until 1944 that it managed to disentangle itself completely from Armstrong's affairs: the final cost, including loss of interest on monies loaned, was almost £1.5 million.

Such difficulties did not deter the Governor, Montagu Norman, from other forays into the world of industrial management and reorganization. As he saw it, some restructuring of British industry was essential, and, if government and the commercial banks were unwilling to take on the job, that left only the Bank of England. Norman's intervention in the affairs of the Lancashire cotton industry in 1928 was justified to the Bank's Committee of Treasury as being necessary 'partly to help the cotton industry, partly to keep the question away from politics, but more especially to relieve certain of the banks from a dangerous position'. (The parlous state of the industry, as has already been noted, was threatening the security of north-western banks such as Williams Deacons.) The industry was restructured and much surplus and outmoded capacity shut down. Shortly afterwards the shipbuilding industry had the same treatment. In these cases the role of the Bank was not as a financier, providing fresh capital, but as a marriage-broker or fixer: under pressure from the Bank, competing companies were persuaded to take a longer-term national view of their industries' futures. But in certain cases the Bank did put its own money into industries in distress. The two famous Cunard liners *Queen Elizabeth* and *Queen Mary* owed something to Norman and the Bank of England: without Bank – and government – money, they would never have been finished.

Norman decided that the Bank's *ad hoc* arrangements needed to be strengthened with the creation of a more formal structure; so he set up Securities Management Trust as a wholly owned Bank of England subsidiary in 1929. Norman described the new company as 'a temporary or industrial adjunct of the Bank of England', and it exists to this day, though now only as a nominee company in which the Bank holds customers' securities. Shortly after, Norman created the Bankers' Industrial Development Company. This existed to foster schemes of industrial reorganization and help such schemes gain financial support. It was wound up during the war.

The generally comfortable economic circumstances of the post-war years meant that this particular part of the Bank's business became unnecessary, and in the fifties and sixties no industrial rescue work of any substance was undertaken. The increasingly serious problems of the British economy in the early 1970s put the problem firmly back on the Bank's agenda. Many industrial companies, trying to keep their heads above water in the complex inflation ridden years of the late sixties and early seventies, found their profitability dropping radically. British industry was ill-equipped to cope with any pressure on its margins.

The immediate cause of the revival of the Bank's rescue business was the dramatic collapse at the beginning of 1971 of one of Britain's most famous names, the engineering giant Rolls Royce. The company was famous for 'making aero engines rather than profits', as its chairman ruefully admitted. What brought it down was the commitment to develop a completely new product, the RB 211 engine, which it had contracted to produce for the American aerospace company Lockheed, for its new Tri-Star airliner. The project proved horrifically expensive, and towards the end of 1970 the company realized that the money was running out. It appealed for help and the Government stumped up £42 million and asked Sir Henry Benson, a senior partner in the accountancy firm of Coopers and Lybrand, to look at the company's finances. Meanwhile the Bank became involved – very much at the last minute – in an attempt to raise a further £30 million of capital in the City. Hardly surprisingly, given the fairly general knowledge of Rolls Royce's problems, it was not an easy task. Aside from that, it was simply too late for effective intervention to save the company.

The Conservative Government decided reluctantly that Rolls Royce would be allowed to go down: this was the only way in which it could be released from its tough contract with Lockheed. Within the Bank there was considerable soul-searching as to why the disaster had happened and how such a major enterprise as Rolls Royce could possibly have drifted onto the rocks without the financial community either being aware of its problems or doing anything about them. Cynics wondered if another underlying reason could also have been of concern to the Bank. There was, at the time, a growing climate of hostility to the City: it was widely felt that the City was 'letting British industry down' by ignoring its needs for money.

A further case which stimulated the Bank's interest in rescue work, and in which it played a rather more productive role, was the collapse of the Burmah Oil company at the end of 1974. Once again everyone was taken by surprise. It was, said one insider, 'literally dropped on our doorstep'. The chairman of Burmah came into the Bank on Christmas Eve, accompanied by his merchant banker, and announced that his firm was bust. Key City figures had to be tracked down from all over the country: one Bank official recalls that, in trying to contact one senior banker, he had to get past an imperious hostess at a party in Norfolk who thought that her guests should not be troubled with business over Christmas. In this case the Bank was able to put an effective rescue package together, and, after some years of convalescence, a slimmed-down Burmah resumed normal trading.

The Rolls Royce episode, and to a lesser extent the collapses of Burmah and other firms, persuaded the then Governor, Gordon Richardson, that he should be prepared for such crises in the future.

He appointed Sir Henry Benson, who had been involved in the Rolls affair, as Industrial Adviser to the Bank. In his new job Benson played a key role in building up the Bank's Industrial Finance Division. Before 1974 virtually no one in the Bank knew much about this area: today the Division has several practitioners skilled in the art of rescue. Its work also involves some twenty to thirty members of the Bank's branch network. David Walker, Executive Director of the Industrial Finance Division, thinks the Bank provides an essential ingredient when it becomes involved in a rescue: 'When a company is in acute financial difficulty, very often there is not a requirement for additional money there and then. Time is needed when the name of the game is survival; the course of action that is needed to ensure survival is very often clear. What's needed is time to implement it.'

The principle behind today's rescues, unlike some of those in the interwar years, is that they do not involve the commitment of the Bank's funds: this is principally and simply because the Bank doesn't have the money for any large-scale support operations for industry. But one cannot help feeling that there is a further reason. The Bank would not wish its freedom of action in this area to be inhibited by having to account to Parliament or the Treasury for any Bank money put at risk in a rescue. This is an area in which speed and discretion are vital, and in most cases the Bank gets to hear of problems before they ever reach the Press or the politicians. The Bank prefers to keep it that way throughout the operation, and in many cases rescues have been completed without news of them ever getting out.

Frequently it is an industrial company's principal banker that first brings the firm's problems to the Bank, asking for help. The reason is not that the bank concerned feels unable to cope; rather it is the increasingly complex pattern of modern industrial finance that is to blame. Large industrial companies operating in several countries tend these days to have numerous bankers: Dunlop, for example, one of the Bank of England's recent 'clients', had some eighty banks involved in its affairs worldwide. The involvement of large numbers of financial backers creates its own problems: as David Walker puts it, 'companies use too many banks ... one creditor may be willing to stay with a company during its difficulty, but almost invariably he will be reluctant to do so unless he's sure that all the other

115

creditors will stay put'. Walker is highly critical of the competitive battle between banks for business: it destroys, as he sees it, the old long-term relationship based on mutual confidence between one bank and one customer. That is not the Bank's only problem: an effective support operation also needs the support of the investing institutions, many of whom do not wish to get involved in the day-to-day affairs of businesses in which they have shares.

The first stage in any rescue is a meeting at the Bank of England of all the creditor banks to discuss the situation. Running such a meeting is a skill, says one insider with experience of them: 'one good way of reaching agreement on these matters is to start the meeting at six o'clock in the evening and throw the key away'. The meeting begins with agreeing a diagnosis. Financial difficulties are usually the symptom of the disease, rather than the disease itself – which may be failure of a new product, marketing problems or managerial difficulties.

The next stage is starting the treatment: the creditor banks are persuaded to appoint a leading firm of accountants to look into the business and make recommendations. Frequently new merchant bankers are appointed as well, on the grounds that a new pair of eyes sometimes sees things differently. One almost invariable requirement is the appointment of new management; and here too the Bank plays a role. It has a little list. As one insider puts it, in a somewhat insouciant fashion, 'one just has to think of people who might be available'. Thus it was that the Bank was able to suggest the name of Sir John Cuckney to Westland Helicopters when that company was in trouble and looking for a new chairman. Cuckney had been the Bank's nominee to sort out the Crown Agents; he followed that with a spell at the Port of London Authority, and then one at the engineering company John Brown. At no stage does the Bank volunteer its own staff for such jobs.

The other key role of the Bank is in keeping the creditors quiet if not happy. 'It is often the small boys who make trouble', explains an insider. The main bank involved probably has no option but to try to keep the business afloat – it may have committed hundreds of millions of pounds in loans already and will be reluctant to throw that away. A small bank, with only marginal commitments of a few millions, will not feel so bound up in the survival of the business. The Bank has ways of making sure that the 'small boys' don't jump

21. Eddie George, Executive Director in charge of Home Finance.

22. David Walker, Executive Director, and Head of the Industrial Finance Division – deeply involved with preparations for Big Bang.

23. 11 a.m. at the
Bank: the daily
'Books' meeting in the
Governor's office.

24. Nigel Althaus, the
Government Broker.

25. The Bank's new gilts dealing room came into operation at Big Bang.

26. The new markets: the London International Financial Futures Exchange, based across the road from the Bank.

27. *The new players: the massive new dealing room of Salomons above Victoria Station.*

ship. The first stage is to take the offender quietly into a back room and explain to him the error of his ways. If this fails other weapons come into play. In some recent cases involving small-town American banks who wanted to pull the rug from under British firms to whom they had lent money, the Bank has asked one of the larger American banks to do its work for it: 'we've asked someone of the standing of Citibank a few times to lean on some small bank in the middle of nowhere that was making trouble', says a Bank man. *In extremis*, the Bank could always turn to its counterpart in America, the Federal Reserve Bank, and ask it to deal with a troublemaker. This technique has been used with Japanese banks in the past – proof that belonging to a club of central bankers has its uses.

Since 1974, a total of some 200 companies have been 'clients' of the Bank in its role of managing industrial rescues. Some have been successes: the restoration to health of Turner and Newall, recently back on the takeover trail, is one; John Brown and Weir are others. And there have been failures: such as the textile engineering group Stone-Platt, which went into receivership despite being rescued by the Bank in 1981. Laker Airways is also seen as a failure: the Bank was involved with that company for months before it went into receivership. But it was a real disaster area, where the prospects for survival were slim, and the Bank only went in, as an insider puts it, to 'pull government's chestnuts out of the fire'.

The level of rescues is now dropping again as industrial profitability rises. At any one time the Bank is now engaged in about half-a-dozen cases. Today's problems are in the oil industry and in related industries such as shipping, which have been hard hit by the collapse in oil prices. The construction industry is a hardy perennial, and a company in this sector can frequently be found in intensive care at the Bank.

On the principle that prevention is better than cure, the Bank puts a lot of effort into taking the pulse of firms that are, with any luck, still healthy. Using its network of branches, the Bank spends a lot of time and money on checking the state of British industry round the country. Each of its branch-managers – who are still known by their old title of 'Agents' – regularly visits some 200–300 companies in his area. These are chosen as being representative of the region. As one of the Agents, Bert Sharples from the Southampton office, puts it, 'I'm a listener to industry, I go out and chat and ask them things like, how do you see the order situation, how are exports doing, is the exchange rate affecting you, is the cash flow all right, are debts getting longer, etc. This is all built up into a picture and I do a report every month.' This report, along with those of other branches, goes to the Bank's Industrial Finance Division.

One might wonder what is in it for the businessmen that help the Agents do this job: according to one of them, Michael Cobham of Flight Refuelling in Dorset, the answer is that it provides a hot line to the top: 'We feel that by telling the Agent our problems and the position we are in, it goes from his desk straight to the Governor on a monthly basis and from the Governor right through to the Treasury and the highest authority.' This information, given in total confidence, adds a valuable dimension to the Bank's economc analysis and is a vital part of its intelligence system.

Given the apparently cloistered and rather inward-looking atmosphere of the Bank, it is something of a surprise to find how well informed its officials are about what is happening in the world outside. The Bank takes pains to ensure that it always has first-class information, whether from industry, commerce or the City. Its officials spend a lot of their time out and about, listening and analysing. As a result, conversation at in-house Bank meetings can be deliciously gossipy, and is peppered with shrewd and knowledgeable comments on what is happening in the big wide world.

That is not the Bank's only source of information: it also puts a lot of effort into strictly economic analysis and the intelligence to be gained from it. It has its own economists, who process mountains of statistical matter each year, and there is a panel of academic consultants who produce learned papers for consideration: a typical recent title is 'The Importance of Interest Rates in Five Macroeconomic Models'. (This group was first set up in 1977 to act as a consultative forum. One of its original members, a contract economist at the Bank, had a rather unfortunate name – Mr Panic.) On top of that, certain executive directors have 'advisers' to help them in policy formulation. Not that the Bank has ever been very keen on academic theory: as Montagu Norman put it to the Macmillan Committee in 1931, 'I do not attach importance to great elaboration of statistical information.' He regarded statistics as 'more valuable for the purpose of testing conclusions arrived at independently than for providing the foundation on which to base conclusions'.

Thirty years later another Governor of the Bank remarked tartly, when urged to have more academic skills in-house, that 'it must be a bank and not a study group'. The Bank set up its Economic Section in 1921. Its staff were encouraged to read 'books and pamphlets on financial and economic subjects' (though only 'out of Bank hours'). At the same time they were warned not to 'become infected with the ideas or the language of an economist'. At the back of this distaste for abstractions is the Bank's long experience in the markets. As Lord Bridges, a Permanent Secretary to the Treasury, put it to a parliamentary committee, the process of policy formulation 'resides in practical wisdom and experience, and not in very clearly thought out theory'.

For that reason the Bank has always respected practical money men from the City. It is these who, from the very beginnings of the Bank, made up its Court of Directors. The Court was, and is, the board of the Bank. It has always been dominated by part-time, non-executive directors. The members in late Victorian times were described by Walter Bagehot as 'plain sensible prosperous English merchants'. They were in effect a self-perpetuating oligarchy, since the Court effectively determined who was to become a member, and thus who in turn would become Governor. He was elected by the Court, and was, till well into this century, an amateur – full-time Governors only arrived in the First World War. The inner cabinet of the Bank is the Committee of Treasury, a sub-committee of the full Court that evolved during the eighteenth century, and which, to this day, exercises some power, although now only over the internal affairs of the Bank. In the nineteenth century it was composed entirely of directors who had, in the curious parlance of the Bank, 'passed the chair' (that is, already been Governor or Deputy). It was memorably described by Bagehot as 'a cabinet of mature, declining and old men'.

The rationale for an amateur board of executives was that its members would bring to bear on the Bank's business their extensive commercial judgement and market knowledge, which would guide the Bank's permanent staff in their duties. The 1946 Act nationalizing the Bank changed little of this, though it removed from the Court the power to elect a Governor. The declaration to be made by new directors of the Bank introduced by the Act gives an indication of

119

what is expected, in theory at least, of a Bank director: the appointee must 'solemnly and sincerely declare that in the said office I will be indifferent and equal to all manner of persons: and I will give my best advice and assistance for the support and good government of the said corporation: and in the execution of the said office I will faithfully and honestly demean myself according to the best of my skill and understanding'. Directors are now appointed by the Government. The Act also broadened the choice of Court-member. Before 1946 the make-up of the Court was overwhelmingly 'City'.

Today's Court has eighteen members, with the Governor, Deputy Governor and four of the Bank's senior executive directors representing the Bank's permanent staff. The remainder are a mix of the City and industry – with some well-known old City names, such as Baring, still represented. The best-known name from industry is Sir Hector Laing, chairman of United Biscuits. A token trade unionist is now also a member of the Court – normally someone on the right of the TUC. Today that role is filled by Gavin Laird, leader of the Amalgamated Union of Engineering Workers.

Laird is pleasantly surprised by the job: 'I thought I was going to be the statutory acceptable figure of trade unionism, expected to come here and have a nice lunch and then go back to my office again – well, you do get a nice lunch, but it's a lot more than that.' He has been impressed by the Bank's role in co-ordinating industrial rescues; although he does admit that he is baffled when financial subjects such as monetary targets come under discussion. Asked whether it is a worthwhile job, he shrugs his shoulders and replies, 'The Court is a bit of icing on the gingerbread. But I still think we do play some kind of a role in advising, or giving an opinion, and hopefully it has an influence on the final decisions the executive make, and hopefully the Government.'

The Governor would never dream of referring to Court as 'icing on the gingerbread', but he agrees it is valuable as a source of advice and support. Significantly, he sees the real power of the Court as a negative one: 'If you sense that the Court is uncertain or against you, then you clearly don't proceed.'

For an observer, the proceedings of the Court are stultifyingly formal and dull. The magnificent surroundings of the Court Room, a loving re-creation of the original design of 1767 (complete with a weathervane indicator so that merchants who were directors could see if ships were likely to dock in the Port of London) lend themselves more to formal speech-making and great occasions than to informal meetings round a table. The acoustics are truly appalling, and those at the far end of the table are fortunate that the present Governor, Robin Leigh-Pemberton, acquired a booming voice during his years in local government. A Governor who muttered would never be heard at the other end of the table.

Some of the business of the Court is a historical record of what has passed and gone. The markets report, given by two executive directors, is effectively ancient history by the time it is delivered. Yesterday is a long time ago in market terms. But there can be matters on which the non-executive Court members can have influence: one such matter, which came up at a recent Court meeting, illustrates both the influence of the Court and the way in which the Bank operates in certain areas with absolutely no formal powers.

The subject was the unlikely one of the Channel Tunnel. This, of course, has absolutely nothing to do with the Bank. But, because the project had run into some trouble with its financing, the Bank felt able to take a hand in matters. The Government had come down in favour of a tunnel as the appropriate fixed link between Britain and Europe, but had stipulated that finance for it must come from the private sector. The victorious consortium, Eurotunnel, set about convincing sceptical investors that a project costing £4700 million and with a payback period of fifty-five years was a good investment. At the end of October, the project ran into trouble raising the first tranche of money, just over £200 million. The City was deeply unimpressed with Eurotunnel's figures. It was at this point that the Bank took action, at the request of the merchant bankers to the project. The Bank took the view, as one senior executive put it to Court, that national pride was at stake: 'It would be troublesome, at least presentationally, for the City if a major long-term national project was not capable of being supported by major financial institutions in circumstances in which the French had committed their portion without, seemingly, any great difficulty.' The Bank made a few 'phone calls and the money appeared, as if by magic. Questioned by the *Sunday Times*, the Bank's official comment was

121

bland in the extreme: 'We were naturally interested, as City institutions were involved. Some discussions took place.'

At the same time, the Bank decided that some more dynamism was needed at the top of Eurotunnel's management, and persuaded the energetic and charismatic Nigel Broakes, chairman of Trafalgar House, to join the board. All this was duly reported to the Bank's Court of Directors. One member, a senior City figure, took the view that the Bank had been somewhat heavy-handed: 'In one case I spoke to, they said they'd never experienced such a weight from the Bank before. Does that worry us?' The Bank's executive directors hastened to reassure the Court that no arm-twisting had been used, and that institutions had clearly been left to make their own commercial decisions. But the executive directors were left in no doubt that the Bank had to tread carefully in applying such pressure, which illustrates the Governor's point about what had to be considered when Court was 'uncertain or against you'.

In that case the Bank was clearly exerting its informal authority within the City. No area of the Bank's operations is more contentious – or perhaps less well documented – than its discreet, and quite unofficial, role as overseer of the City. Newspapers have devoted acres of newsprint, and many hours of speculation, to exploring the 'nods and winks' of the Bank; they have worried endlessly over whether, in some particular case, the 'eyebrows' of the Governor have been raised or not. The Bank declines to comment on any such cases, and, on the whole, so does the person or institution on the receiving end of the 'nod and wink'.

Insiders seem to get almost indecent delight from befuddling outsiders in their pursuit of knowledge on this subject. The Deputy Governor, George Blunden, grinned broadly as he recalled the former Governor of the Bank who, 'whenever he heard people talking about "nods and winks", got a picture of himself sitting in a chair as a gibbering idiot'. More seriously, Mr Blunden went on to define the process in rather more Bank-like language: 'We sit, with a degree of detachment, watching what people are doing. They come to us, we give them advice. The advice we give should be good advice, if we're doing our jobs properly, and they will take notice of it.' But what if they don't take notice? For those, such as other banks, who come directly under the Bank's statutory powers, the ultimate sanction is the law; with some others, the Bank has, as the Deputy Governor puts it, 'a degree of power over people's ability to do business'. Asked what he would do with those who nevertheless ignored the Bank's advice, he replied, 'I find it hard to recognize that situation.'

The point about the Bank's informal power is expanded by the Governor: 'The Bank exercises great influence on the markets and that influence becomes something not far short of power, because people cannot afford, from the point of view of their market position, to offend us too much.' By this he means that traders in the market, such as discount houses, who deal with the Bank on a daily basis cannot afford to have the privilege of doing that business – or being 'accommodated', as the phrase has it – withdrawn. But authority is not always a matter of power: in cases where no sanctions of any sort can be applied, the Bank must, as one insider puts it, 'persuade people of the rightness of our views. When the Bank does say something ... then people do assume that it has been carefully thought through and is worth thinking about themselves.'

The Governor regards the statement of such carefully thought out views as being of value to all: 'They like our advice and they accept it because they see that it is in their interests to maintain that sort of stability, the sort of standards that they've associated with the Bank's influence and authority over the years. I make no shame about pleading that in these new markets people should still accept the spirit of the situation and not too readily resort to the legalistic side of it.'

Bank executive director David Walker hopes that the influence of the Governor's eyebrows will survive the new age: many of the new players in the market are very happy, he says, to come and talk to the Bank about what they are doing: 'The reason, in a nutshell, is that outside the Bank most of the people they deal with are either customers or competitors ... and when they come here they're talking to people who are knowledgeable about their market but who are disinterested.' David Scholey, head of Mercury Securities, one of the City's new financial conglomerates, and a director of the Bank, thinks that the Bank still retains enormous authority: 'If the Governor or Deputy Governor felt – and their antennae are very sensitive – that there was something going on that might be of interest to them, and they were not being informed of it directly by us, they wouldn't hesitate to ask us to step down the road and explain what was going on.' That didn't happen as the Mercury group was being put together, precisely because Scholey didn't relish a summons to the Bank out of the blue: instead he kept the Bank informed of what was going on in what he describes as 'a very confessional way'. He made sure that he told the Bank 'what was on our minds, not necessarily so they would say yes or no, but so that they would have the opportunity to express views of approval or disapproval or indeed make constructive proposals'.

And there are plenty of similar stories about the Bank's subtle power-plays. One director of a major City merchant bank was astonished that anyone should think that the Governor's eyebrows were no longer a force to be reckoned with: he had been summoned, with several of his colleagues, to what turned out to be a very sticky interview with the Deputy Governor after his firm had proposed going into a new and, in the Bank's eyes, somewhat unsuitable area of business: 'We were kept cooling our heels in one of those elegant little waiting rooms off the parlours. We had long enough to read the back numbers of Country Life a couple of times before we were hauled in to be told in the politest of terms that what we wanted to do was not on.' The bank complied and withdrew its proposal.

The Bank is, however, by no means unchallenged in its exercise of informal power. The power is only effective when no one chooses to challenge it or when it is exercised over those clearly within the Bank's control. When there was a battle over ownership of a Scottish clearing bank in 1981, the Bank ended up looking – and in effect being – ineffective. A British overseas bank, the Hongkong and Shanghai Bank, made a contested bid for the Royal Bank of Scotland group. The Bank of England did not approve. It dislikes contested bids in the banking sector, and was not too happy that a British clearer should be acquired by a bank from freewheeling Hong Kong, a place in which it has no authority and where there is no effective banking supervision. On top of that, the highly competitive and market-oriented HKSB group, described with some pleasure by its then chairman Michael Sandberg as 'the yellow peril', could introduce some undesirable aspects into British banking. But the Bank had, at the time, no powers to do anything about it, and was only saved from an embarrassing public demonstration of its impotence by a referral of the bid to the Monopolies Commission. This ruled that the public interest would not be served by the bid going ahead. The new Banking Act gives the Bank powers to intervene in takeovers – but only on 'prudential' (that is to say, strictly supervisory) grounds.

On another recent occasion the role of the Bank in interpreting the new Banking Act provided an opportunity for the Governor's eyebrows to be more successfully raised. The Bank, like many in the City, was worried at the acquisition of a large stake in David Scholey's firm, Mercury Securities, by the colourful American financier Saul Steinberg. It was widely felt that his coming to run a major house in London would not be welcomed in the City. The Bank could not say so publicly, but took advantage of Press inquiries about the precise terms of the new Banking Act to point out that the new Act gave it powers, as banking supervisor, to stop control of banks changing hands, where there were 'prudential' grounds for such intervention. The Press duly linked this comment to speculation about Mr Steinberg's stake in Mercury. In the late autumn of 1986 this stake was sold, amid sighs of relief in the City. No one knows whether what the Bank said, and the Press interpreted, had any impact on the decision to sell.

Declining to raise your eyebrows can be more effective than using them. When the American giant Citibank tried to muscle in on the highly profitable and protected British market, the Bank of England could be seen as having, if not helped the application, certainly not hindered it. Citibank was keen to move up into the front line of British banking and become a major player. The British clearing banks were unhappy at the idea of further competition for retail deposits, and lobbied long and hard for Citibank to be discouraged in some way. The Bank, echoing the Conservative Government's belief that competition is good for you, declined to take a stand in any way. Eventually the disgruntled clearers were forced to admit Citibank to their own clearing system.

In the political world, the Bank is clearly seen as being less influential in the City than it once was; but, then, the politicians by their words and actions have done much to undermine the standing of the Bank. In particular, the way in which the politicians have striven to make the Bank their creature rather than the City's has weakened the Bank's authority. At the same time the effectiveness in representing the views of the City to Whitehall has lessened. As a result the Bank has lost, over the last few years, its role as a middleman: no longer is it the spokesman of government to the City and of the City to government. Nowadays it is increasingly seen as the Government's agent in the City.

Ironically it is the Tories who have recently done the most damage to the Bank's standing. Former Treasury minister Jock Bruce-Gardyne explains: 'What the City regarded as the most disgraceful affront perpetrated on it in recent years was the decision to impose a levy on bank profits in the 1981 Budget.' There's no doubt the City felt that the Governor, in failing to prevent that from happening, let them down. And in 1984 a further assault by the Chancellor on the banks – in the form of closing a loophole that had enabled them to increase their reserves painlessly by entering the leasing business – meant that the image of the Bank of England in the eyes of its fellow banks was more tarnished than ever.

At the same time as government was devaluing the position of the Bank in the City, another of the Bank's traditional roles, that of helping the City to manage itself without help from government, also appeared to be increasingly fraught with difficulty. Traditionally the City has preferred to run its own affairs, free from any government intervention or supervision. This has been supported at the Bank, which for many years has vigorously preached the virtues of self-regulation. This is now coming increasingly under attack from Westminster, and even from within certain parts of the City itself.

A good example of the changing times are the current wrangles over the status of the Takeover Panel. This is a uniquely British creation, an organization that has no statutory powers behind it and is not, indeed, authorized by anyone. It was set up in 1968 as a result of public disquiet about the spate of takeovers then taking place. It was very much a creation of the Bank – a small informal outfit, staffed by City insiders, and able to move fast when circumstances required it to. At the time the City agreed to abide by the decisions of the Panel. For many years its quite unsupported authority worked well: the founding chairman, Lord Shawcross, was famous for his dressing-downs of merchant bankers who failed to meet his demands.

Recently, though, the whole takeover business has been back in the news again. 1985 and 1986 saw massive new bids announced almost weekly. Such activity is cyclical: at times when some companies have plenty of cash and others are enfeebled, buying market position by taking over a company can make a lot of sense. It is estimated that, in the first three quarters of 1986 alone, the value of all takeovers successfully completed exceeded £10,000 million, with several more large ones in the pipeline at the end of the period. The scale of the business soon had the Bank worried that it was getting out of hand. In March 1986 the Governor of the Bank expressed his doubts about the frenzy of bidding and dealing: apart from worries that predator companies were burdening themselves with too much debt, Mr Leigh-Pemberton also felt that the atmosphere in the City was getting a little unhealthy: 'Competitive pressures have bred in some younger people in the City ... a keener edge and a tendency to be a little more cavalier towards the regulations.'

At the same time the Panel came under attack for not limiting the excesses of takeover fever: it did introduce new rules banning vitriolic advertising in bid battles, but did not succeed in lowering the temperature in any other way. Critics wondered how long the gentlemanly agreement to abide by the decisions of the Panel would survive in a more competitive era where the stakes would be much higher. This lack of confidence in the Panel spread to participants in takeovers too. Autumn 1986 saw a bitter battle for the control of the printing firm McCorquodale. In the course of it the Panel gave a ruling that angered Prudential-Bache, the American securities firm that was advising one of the firms involved. Rather than accept the decision with good grace, as was customary, Pru-Bache promptly appealed against the ruling in the courts – the first time the authority of the Takeover Panel had ever been tested in a law court. The Master of the Rolls, Sir John Donaldson, summed up the problem by asking, 'Have we got a rogue power centre [the Takeover Panel] which is wholly unsusceptible to any form of control by the courts?' He concluded that this was not the case, and that the decisions of the Panel could be challenged in the courts, although he anticipated a 'workable and valuable partnership between the court and the panel in the public interest'. *The Times* described this judgement as 'the possible deathknell of self-regulation' and speculated on 'the inevitable arrival in Britain of increased litigation as a way to resolve corporate battles'.

In the City too, critics have attacked the role of the Takeover Panel. In the recent battle for the control of the engineering firm

AE, the Panel was accused of 'pursuing blinkered City interest' in not looking more closely at the industrial logic behind the battle. This was hardly a fair criticism – the Panel is not there to make such judgements – but it is a sign of the times that City opinion is now looking beyond the immediate financial implications of bids and deals to the rationale behind them, and wants the Takeover Panel to do the same. A *Times* editorial suggested that it was time to overhaul the code on takeovers, arguing that the continuing 'abuse of power of finance over industry' needed examination. The paper suggested that 'the Bank of England might here again take a lead'. The revelations of the ineffectiveness of the Panel during the Guinness takeover battle have clinched the argument. It is now clear that during that struggle the guidelines of the Panel were blatantly flouted. As a result, the Government has announced that it will be conducting urgent discussions with the city regulatory authorities – including the Bank – on the role and rules of the Takeover Panel.

In other areas of its self-imposed role as village bobby in the City, the Bank has had its problems. It has played a major role in cleaning up the mess at the Lloyds insurance market. This is not the place to recall in detail the many disasters that have befallen Lloyds; a catalogue of poor management, inadequate regulation, incompetence and sheer criminal behaviour produced a situation in which it was possible for a large number of frauds to be perpetrated against the so-called 'names' – wealthy individuals who are outside Lloyds but underwrite the business conducted there. The Bank ensured that it was invited to involve itself in the affairs of Lloyds in the early 1980s, on the grounds that these scandals were shaking public confidence in the market. The Bank insisted that more professional management was required, and turned, as it often does in such circumstances, to the accountancy profession to provide this. Lloyds was persuaded to accept this solution, and in February 1983 Ian Hay Davison, a partner in the accounting firm Arthur Andersen, arrived to sort out the mess.

The Bank had already delivered its side of this bargain by persuading the Conservative Government to leave Lloyds to sort out its own affairs. This was effectively enshrined in law in the Lloyds Act of 1982. But the affair has not proved a simple one for the Bank; the insurance market still seems to be in as much of a mess as it ever was. Recently there have been further serious scandals involving

128

Lloyds – one massive case, involving potential losses to 'names' of some £380 million over the next two decades, is still being argued about. These cases have led to yet another inquiry. The latest report on the state of affairs inside Lloyds – the Neill Report, published in January 1987 – proposed yet more reforms, some 70 in all, to restore the good name of the insurance market. But this time it seems that the authorities are taking little on trust: the Government has clearly warned that if these latest changes do not succeed in cleaning up the market, legislation to do so will follow. The Bank has also made it clear that this time Lloyds will be on its own, and must make the reforms work.

However serious the challenges posed by Lloyds and similar cases to the informal exercise of the Bank of England's powers, such episodes are almost insignificant compared to the dangers posed by the revolution that is now sweeping through the City's financial markets – Big Bang. Trying to sort out the problems of the insurance market, even the problems of ailing British companies, is easy work compared to the high drama involved in turning upside-down the way that the City of London has done its main business for well over a century. It is a drama that the Bank of England is at the heart of; and the success or failure of it will determine London's place in the financial world of the future.

8

The Caravan Moves On: Big Bang and the Bank

Just before 3.30 p.m. on 24 October 1986 the distinguished figure of the government broker, Nigel Althaus, stepped out of the Bank of England and walked 150 yards round the corner for one of his regular visits to the Stock Exchange. He was following a long tradition of making such calls – when the Exchange opened, from time to time during the day, and just before it closed in the afternoon. He moved from pitch to pitch in the corner of the floor that traded in gilts, British government securities. This time Mr Althaus, wearing the traditional silk top hat, was bringing with him news of a major issue of stock designed to show the Bank's confidence in the Stock Exchange as it entered the brave new world of Big Bang.

Normally the government broker is received on the floor of the Exchange with the respect due to his position as one of the major figures in the market. This particular afternoon, however, was different. It was the last trading day before the upheaval of Big Bang, and market dealers had clearly decided that, if the world was going to end, then better with a bang than a whimper. Celebrations of the end of an age had been going on since lunchtime; the rules of the Exchange banning drink on the floor had been blatantly ignored. (There must also be a rule that people dressed up as donkeys are forbidden on the floor; if so, that was flouted too.) Mr Althaus, as a representative of the old order, received an uproarious welcome.

The fact that he was accompanied by a film crew as he moved in stately procession around the floor cannot have helped. Within minutes he was surrounded by a huge crowd of cheering and singing people; streamers were thrown, poppers exploded and the crowd burst into singing. Their choice of songs seemed to indicate both the excitement and the uncertainties generated by Big Bang. First they gave a spirited rendition of an old footballing favourite, 'Here we go, here we go, here we go ...' This was followed, rather more sombrely, by Auld Lang Syne. Meanwhile the more high-spirited had helped themselves to Mr Althaus's top hat and were passing it from hand to hand above the crowd. Nigel Althaus himself took it all in good part, remarking with a smile that 'things seem a little lively today'. As he left the floor, numerous people came to shake his hand and wish him well in his new career as a public servant.

Before Big Bang, Nigel Althaus was the senior partner of Mullens, who have been since 1786 the Government's brokers (or, as they are more correctly termed, Brokers to the Commissioners for the Reduction of the National Debt, a somewhat optimistic job description). But in all that time Mullens remained an independent firm. One of the smaller upheavals of Big Bang was that certain of Mullens' staff became Bank of England employees, Nigel Althaus among them. (The rest of the firm was absorbed by Mercury Securities – the new name for Warburgs – at the instigation, so it is said, of the Bank of England.)

Many people have claimed to be the inspirer of Big Bang; but in reality, like most revolutions, it had no parents – arising as it did out of a gradually changing set of circumstances in the marketplace – but plenty of godparents. The Bank of England was one of those, albeit that its role was a hidden one most of the time, performed behind the scenes. It might seem strange to regard the Bank as an institution abetting a revolution: it is more usual in the City to see it as the upholder of the old ways, as the opponent of reform and change. But such a view is rather short-sighted and narrow. As with so much else that involves the Bank of England, to understand what happens today you must understand what has already happened: the historical perspective. To see why the Bank should have forced the upheaval of Big Bang on the City, it is necessary both to look back to the time when London was the genuinely open and competitive centre of the world's financial markets, and to take account of the global changes in the money business that have taken place in recent years and made Big Bang inevitable.

During the nineteenth century Britain was the centre of world trade, with more than half of it being financed in sterling. That in turn led to such businesses as the insurance and commodities markets being centred on London. On top of that the City of London was, overwhelmingly, the source of the world's development capital. At its peak, in 1913, over half of British savings went into foreign investment. And underlining London's key role as financial centre of the world was the sheer strength of the British industrial economy.

The decline in Britain's status as an industrial power by the end of the First World War initially had little impact on the City; much of its business survived the crumbling of the economic strength of the industrial sector. But it was clear by the twenties that world leadership of the financial sector was passing, as industrial supremacy had a generation earlier, to the United States. Britain was forced into a secondary position. The abandonment of the gold standard and the adoption of a subordinate role for sterling had the effect of reducing the City's importance in key world financial markets. It was the fervent ambition of the Bank of England to reverse this decline in the City's fortunes: underlying many of the actions of the Bank's longest-serving Governor, Montagu Norman, was the hope that he would live to see the City of London restored to its primacy in the financial world. In one of his rare public speeches, at the Mansion House dinner in 1933, while acknowledging that immediate prospects were grim, he warned the City that the old order was changing and that the City could not ignore change in the world financial scene. To those who might oppose such changes, he ended his speech with a dark threat that managed to upset many in his audience: 'the dogs may bark, but the caravan moves on'.

Another world war saw the caravan move on at a greater speed, with Britain, and particularly the City of London, left even further behind. The damage done by the mass of German bombs that had rained down on the Square Mile seemed to symbolize a general collapse of the City's standing in the world. During the years after the war London steadily lost power and influence as other centres advanced. While half of world trade had been financed in sterling before the war, by the mid-sixties that had declined to 25 per cent. At the same time, recurrent British financial crises and devaluations also weakened the City's position enormously. A final blow to

132

London in the post-war years was the gradual disappearance of the sterling area – a useful bonus that had brought much business London's way.

The turnaround in the City's fortunes that stopped this decline owes much to the benign neglect of the Bank of England; a case in which what the Bank did was less important than what it did not do. The Bank's generally rather easy-going attitudes made London an ideal centre for various new forms of financial business that found the highly regulated environment of New York distasteful. The process has been nicknamed 'The Tale of Two Cities'. Effectively the Bank permitted the development of a parallel economy in the City, alongside the traditional one, but an economy which grew at somewhat greater speed. The barrier separating the two was sterling exchange controls, which operated until 1979. The domestic financial economy remained firmly under the Bank's control: this was the part subject to exchange controls, which of course were run by the Bank. The other economy of the City, the international one as it were, was much more loosely regulated by the Bank; but, since it dealt predominantly in financial instruments denominated in currencies other than sterling, its operations had little domestic impact.

Soon London became the centre of a number of new markets. Perhaps the best known is the Eurodollar market, which grew up during the sixties. This had its origins in the large pool of dollars held outside the United States which the owners – mainly large US multinationals – did not wish to repatriate: America had a number of rules which controlled domestic interest rates and forced banks to hold some of their reserves in non-interest-bearing deposits. The owners of these dollars wanted to find someone outside America to lend them to. Bankers in London, British and foreign, started a market in this new offshore currency; a market that has grown from a few hundred million dollars a year in the early sixties to more than $300 billion now. As a result by the end of the seventies there were more American banks in London than in New York; overall the number of foreign banks in London trebled between 1970 and 1980. It must be emphasized that this market had little or nothing to do with the British economy; it was a completely offshore business, dealing in a currency upon which there were effectively no controls. The same could be said of many of the other new markets that grew up at the same time. Banks found London a convenient place to conduct a great variety of international business, and soon a vast array of new financial instruments were being devised, packaged and traded through London.

Lord Rothschild used to say, when working at the family bank, that banking 'consists essentially of facilitating the movement of money from point A, where it is, to point B, where it is needed'. Bankers, however, hate anything so simple, and have accordingly developed exotic names for the bewildering new range of financial packages they have devised in recent years: certificates of deposit, floating-rate notes, syndicated loans, and so on. Markets in all of these have found a home in London. By 1979, for example, 63 per cent of all syndicated loans – by then a business turning over $80 billion a year – were organized in London.

On the surface, then, it looked as if there was no need to make any alteration to London's financial structure: many in the late seventies thought that Britain had managed to get the best of both worlds. But a careful look at the balance sheet of the City revealed that the liabilities outweighed the assets. On the credit side, Britain had five of the world's twenty largest banks, a strong and profitable insurance sector (comprising both individual companies and Lloyd), and a number of highly skilled merchant banks with good international reputations. On top of that, London had a large share of the world's money and commodity traders.

The debit side was less visible, but none the less highly damaging. London's Stock Exchange was hopelessly outmoded and becoming an also-ran in international terms (at the time of the shift towards Big Bang, it was only just bigger than the Frankfurt exchange; and in a survey of British fund managers it was discovered that only 5 per cent of their Japanese, Canadian or Australian investments were made through a firm belonging to the Stock Exchange); Britain's major banks were running out of prospects for growth, and were in danger of losing their place in the world ranking (principally because of Britain's less than dynamic economic performance); while the City's merchant banks were clearly losing business to better capitalized and more powerful competitors abroad. At the same time the Lloyds insurance market was seeing a steady decline in its share of world business, and some of the other specialist markets based in London – such as commodities and shipping – were beginning to look very old-fashioned and uncompetitive in an age of fast on-screen electronic trading.

What was happening to the City was what had happened, over the years, to British manufacturing industry. Industry had failed to face the challenge of new rivals abroad, properly capitalized, equipped with the latest technology, and capable of effective marketing. In the same way the City had not responded to the challenge from overseas to its traditional leadership. It had caught the British disease of a narrow islander's view of the world.

It is very difficult to put a finger on what caused the change in City attitudes to a more internationalist viewpoint. Certainly it preceded Big Bang by some years. One factor was the rising quantity of offshore financial business discussed earlier. From being seen at the end of the sixties as a sort of froth on the serious business of domestic banking, international business became the key to growth in the early seventies. For this the Arabs must bear much of the credit.

The fourfold rise in oil prices in 1973 created a dramatic problem for the Arab oil-producing nations: what to do with the vast quantities of money they were now generating. With minute populations there was no way they could spend the money: it had to be invested. At the time, the *Economist* magazine calculated that the two richest producers, Saudi Arabia and Kuwait, would be able to buy all the stock of IBM with just seven months' oil revenues, and the whole of Exxon with a mere four months' money. Since the world's formal monetary machinery, such as the International Monetary Fund and the World Bank, was incapable of dealing with such huge sums, the job of recycling oil wealth fell to the commercial banks. In the process, the major banks were transformed, willy-nilly, into multinational businesses. As Walter Wriston, the head of the American banking giant Citicorp, put it, 'It was the greatest transfer of wealth in the shortest time frame and with the least casualties in the history of the world.... It was a technically difficult thing to do. We did it. It was also hard to put the guy on the moon. We did that.'

The problem behind such brave words was that it was very difficult to find suitable homes for the money. Industrialized countries were reeling from the recession brought on by the impact of higher oil prices. So the banks instead placed the money with what were then euphemistically known as developing countries: Third World nations that were desperate for development capital to help them grow out of poverty. In the process many of the banks came close to ruin, because they collectively forgot the basic rules of sound banking practice. Even those who behaved sensibly came close to the abyss. As the economist John Maynard Keynes had put it many years before, 'a "sound" banker alas, is not one who foresees ruin and avoids it, but one who, when he is ruined, is ruined in a conventional and orthodox way along with his fellows, so that no one can really blame him'.

The banks rushed to invest in the developing world, not out of any misguided sense of charity, but because it was very profitable: in 1974, for example, Citicorp earned 40 per cent of its profits from loans to the Third World – loans that were only 7 per cent of its assets. The banks thought they had invented a means of printing money. The loans were risky, which meant steep rates of interest (good for the bottom line), but not that risky: after all, the bankers reasoned, the borrowers were sovereign states, and as such they could never default. By 1977 the developing countries owed the banks $75 billion.

Much of the money vanished *en route* into private bank accounts; more found its way into absurd and prestigious projects that could never have been justifiable on any grounds whatever. A hopelessly backward and corrupt African state such as Zaire found itself courted by bankers – its government was, after all, pro-Western – and launched into a massive programme of investment in its infra-structure: this included a steel works, prompting one banker to remark, 'Zaire needs a steelworks like it needs central heating.' By 1976 Zaire was in hock to the tune of $400 million: small beer compared to some, but money the country could never afford to pay back.

All around the world, the story was the same: too much bor-rowing followed by a repayments crisis, during which the one word that was never used was 'default'. Whatever else happened, the big banks were reluctant to allow any of their loans – which of course were listed in their books as an asset – to be judged as non-performing as a result of default. (Default would turn these assets into liabilities and thus undermine the banks' balance sheets.) In many cases new money was lent to keep up the illusion that developing nations could get themselves out of the mire of debt. Country after country got into trouble: several African nations led the way, followed by Indonesia and some Eastern European countries, such as Poland. After that it was the turn of the big Latin American borrowers, with crises in Brazil, Peru, Argentina and Mexico. Those crises are still going on: sorting out Mexico's debt problems is one of the world's few growth industries. By the end of 1985 it was calculated that more than thirty countries, with total debts of almost $300 billion were in arrears on repayments or had rescheduled their debts.

All of this meant that by the beginning of the eighties the banks had been frightened off the business of lending to Third World governments and had to find other avenues for expansion. As many faced effective saturation of banking services in their own home markets, this left international lending to blue-chip companies and Western governments as the only avenue to growth. Such lending was highly competitive, and the banks found the market under attack from two directions: on the one hand new financial middle-men were coming on the scene, able to put together deals between companies that eliminated traditional banks. They added a new word to the financial vocabulary: 'securitization'. This is the process whereby long-term debt from companies and others is packaged by a finance house and sold on to investors, who in return receive income from it. This debt is effectively marketed like any other security. (One jealous rival said of one of the pioneers of these new marketing techniques, the American giant Salomons, that 'They'd try birth and death certificates if they could make a market.')

At the same time traditional customers were becoming much more sophisticated, and, armed with a battery of new technology, were stripping away much of the mystique of banking. As a result, in the last few years bank lending has dropped away dramatically, while the international bond market has taken off. Together these factors ensured that what had been a series of separate, though interconnected, marketplaces around the world became one global trading zone. In essence that meant that no major financial institution could think of itself in anything but an international way.

The smart customer is a fairly recent phenomenon. In the immediate post-war years, manufacturing companies designed and made things and got their banks to finance the production and marketing

137

of them. There was a clear distinction between making things and handling money. The growth of massive multinational companies – the IBMs and the BPs of the world – inevitably affected this neat division of labour. Multinationals had to manage their affairs in several countries at once, with funds being moved from place to place as required. This meant that they had to understand the workings of various foreign-exchange markets round the world, so that money could be transferred at the strategic moment from one currency to another. (When the headlines talk of speculative pressure on sterling, they are referring, at least in part, to corporate treasurers of large companies who are making sure that they are not exposed to fluctuations in the sterling rate.) But multinationals are now involved in more than just foreign-exchange operations. Many companies are in the money markets too. In the old days, excess funds were simply put on deposit at the bank: today corporate treasurers are big players in the money markets on their own account, and trade money and commercial paper just like any bank.

Technology has helped this to happen, much of it provided by the banks themselves. For example, in the early eighties Citicorp offered its corporate customers a sophisticated system of cash management which gave the corporate treasurer a desk-top microcomputer linked into Citicorp's worldwide data network. Using this the treasurer was able to check on the state of corporate accounts round the world at the push of a button: payments could be authorized, and funds moved from one country to another, in seconds. Banks were ceasing to be places to keep money, and becoming instead the means through which it could be managed. As Walter Wriston put it, in a famous phrase, 'the information standard has replaced the gold standard as the basis of world finance'. It is significant that Citicorp has announced that its competitors in the 1990s will not be other banks, but IBM, American Telephone and Telegraph, and Reuters. Of course the sheer speed of technological change means that such systems of cash management, which in the early eighties only huge companies could afford, are today the basis of home electronic banking.

It is this technological revolution that is at the heart of the logic of Big Bang. The merging of the technology of the telephone and the computer means that physical presence, the face-to-face contact of traders, is no longer necessary. It is fast being replaced in almost

138

every type of market by what is called screen dealing. The trader can see prices quoted on a monitor, with details of trades and spreads between bid and offer prices (all updated electronically). He then does his trading over the 'phone. The necessary confirmation and paperwork are done swiftly by computer. The formidable strengths of such a system are illustrated by the meteoric rise of Reuters, once a rather dull news-agency operation, to superstar status as an international company. In 1973 Reuters introduced a financial screen service called Reuter Monitor, which provided traders with up-to-date prices. This proved spectacularly successful and within ten years Reuters had some 40,000 screens installed in forty-one countries. (By 1986, the number had almost doubled again.)

In some markets, screens were the only basis of dealing: the American National Association of Securities Dealers introduced a system called NASDAQ in 1971, which linked traders together in a network spanning America. By 1985 NASDAQ had more than 120,000 dealers on its system, with a turnover of more than 16 billion shares valued at $200 billion. This made NASDAQ the third-largest share market in the world after New York and Tokyo. Conventional stock exchanges, such as London and most of the European exchanges, which dealt on a face-to-face basis, were fast being left behind. The speed and efficiency of screen dealing has been shown by the swift demise of the old way of doing things in London: today the floor of the Stock Exchange is almost deserted, and it looks as if the last fling of the floor traders will prove to have been the opening of trading in British Gas shares at the beginning of December 1986.

The replacement of face-to-face trading by screen dealing means, of course, that the various parties to a trade can be anywhere in the world where there is a telephone line. That posed an immense threat to traditional markets such as London – and it is clear that technology would have forced Big Bang even if other factors had not. The other side of the electronics revolution is the instantaneity of news. Information which influences the markets can now travel so fast that any dealer not equipped to process it immediately is at a disadvantage. This has also had a major impact on the City, because the technology is expensive and requires massive capital investment. One British firm, Kleinwort Grieveson, invested around £12 million in a screen-dealing system with a response time of five seconds. The firm had thought of getting ahead of rivals by cutting that response time to just one second, but rejected the idea on the grounds that the extra speed was not worth the extra millions – it would have cost another £24 million.

Massive investment such as this in turn required large businesses with big capital backing. Another factor that made Big Bang inevitable was the growth of new and powerful financial institutions operating on a world scale, offering a full range of services across a broad front. Here again Britain was way behind the game. Too many of the country's financial institutions were simply too small in terms of capital base, and had failed to follow the example of overseas rivals. In the early 1970s America's main investment banks were similar in size to Britain's merchant banks. (Despite the difference in terminology, both do essentially the same thing.) The Americans went through the process of deregulation – it was known there as Mayday – in 1975, and the result was a wave of mergers and acquisitions which produced a handful of much larger financial institutions. Weaker firms went to the wall. The capital base of a leading firm such as Merrill Lynch was, by Big Bang, ten times that of most London merchant banks. The same could be said of most firms in the sector: Britain's financial businesses were too fragmented and small, too dependent on controlled markets and specialist niches.

All these factors have forced an opening up of the main financial markets round the globe. America led the way with the ending of all foreign-exchange controls followed by Mayday on Wall Street in the mid-seventies. In London exchange controls were abolished in 1979, thus ending 'The Tale of Two Cities'; full-scale deregulation followed on from the Stock Exchange's agreement in 1983 to dismantle its restrictive practices. In this instance, Tokyo is still behind London and New York: major steps to loosen controls over markets there are only just beginning.

But Japan will be a formidable rival in the years to come. The sheer size and energy of the country's economy, and Japan's immense skill at entering other people's markets, shown already in the industrial field, mean that Japanese financial conglomerates are bound to be a major threat. The main Japanese securities houses are very big and very profitable: Nomura, the largest, which handles 15 per cent of Japanese share transactions, made a pre-tax profit four times that of Barclays Bank in the year to December 1985. Backing Japan's drive to dominate world financial markets are some immense generators of money. For example, Japan's Post Office Savings Bank is a formidable institution in a country whose tax laws encourage saving: its deposits of $580 billion are six times larger than Citicorp's. At the moment this money has to be invested with the Japanese Ministry of Finance; but soon that restriction will end, and further massive funds will be loosed onto the world market. Not that the Japanese are not there already in force: it is estimated that half the London interbank market funds now come from Japanese banks.

This was the background against which the Office of Fair Trading (OFT) investigation into the restrictive practices of the Stock Exchange began at the behest of the incoming Conservative Government at the end of the seventies. At first sight this seemed to many City observers a small matter of an interfering government watchdog trying to upset the habits of generations past. In essence the action was based on the fact that many of the practices of the Stock Exchange were patently restrictive in their effects on trade, and were thus against the public interest. A government committed to increasing Britain's competitiveness could not ignore them. From such limited beginnings the whole affair snowballed, eventually turning into the massive upheaval of Big Bang. The Bank of England played a large part in this snowball effect. Its initial reaction to the OFT case had been to argue the traditional City view that such matters were best sorted out by City insiders rather than Whitehall. When it became clear that this was not acceptable to the politicians, the Bank began to take a rather more in-depth look at the matter and concluded that, if wholesale change was required, it had better be managed change rather than chaos.

It would be easy to argue that this was a natural and thought-out progression from Montagu Norman's hopes, as Governor in the twenties and thirties, that the City could regain its international leadership by opening its markets to the world's traders. Bank insiders insist that this was not the case. There was, they say, no premeditation in the actions the Bank took to ensure a transition to a more competitive marketplace. The Bank's interest in the matter was twofold: it regarded the Stock Exchange as part of its general City bailiwick, and therefore resented outsiders telling the Exchange how to run its affairs; more important, as the biggest single customer of the Stock Exchange – via its gilts operations – it had a vested interest in ensuring an effective marketplace for government securities.

The job of providing the City with leadership fell to one of the Bank's executive directors, David Walker, a former Treasury economist who had moved to the Bank in Gordon Richardson's time. Walker's principal activity was running the Industrial Finance Division of the Bank. With the improvement in the finances of British industry in the eighties, and thus fewer industrial lifeboat cases, he had, as he puts it, 'time on his hands'. As befits a man who has had Whitehall training, David Walker is an avowed interventionist in economic matters, and decided that the Bank should take the lead in convincing the City of the need for internal reform. As he puts it now, 'It seemed to us important that, if there were to be any chance that London would be a significant international capital market centre, the Stock Exchange must be helped and encouraged to escape from its rather locked-in mood. Unless we ... in government and in the Bank of England and the Stock Exchange were able, to put it crudely, to get our act together ... there was a risk that the UK securities industry would go the way of some other British industries.'

The Bank accordingly proposed to Whitehall that, if the Government dropped the case against the Stock Exchange, the Bank would ensure that the Exchange thoroughly reformed its undesirable practices over a specific period of time. In summer 1983 the Bank finally managed to convince government, and the famous deal was struck between the Trade Secretary, Cecil Parkinson, and the chairman of the Stock Exchange, Sir Nicholas Goodison. It gave the Exchange just over three years to 27 October 1986 – Big Bang day – to put its house in order.

Few in the City appreciated how significant a process that was to be. Many thought that with a bit of luck life would go on much as before: indeed, even at the time of the deal, many in the Stock Exchange believed that it would be quite possible to retain the principle of single capacity (that is to say, the separation of jobbers, the market makers, and brokers, the dealers). The Bank saw from the start that this could not be, and made its views clear to the Stock Exchange. If there was to be reform, it would have to go the whole way. The City had to be persuaded that a fundamental revolution was taking place which would end with London operating in the same way as New York and competing with it and Tokyo for business. The Governor, Robin Leigh-Pemberton, put it bluntly in a speech at the time: 'it is not open to us simply to choose the best market system for our domestic purposes, without regard to the realities of the outside world'. The Bank realized that the logic of making the Exchange competitive meant that there would have to be a system of trading which involved large market-making firms. No existing London jobbing firm had the capital to be a large-scale market maker – that is to say, hold large blocks of shares on its books – and that in turn meant letting outsiders, including foreign firms, own market makers. Only in this way could sufficient funds be drawn in to support the operations of the market. This meant that what looked like a few small changes had in reality to be much more dramatic in scope. It would mean, as it had in New York, a wave of mergers and acquisitions before Big Bang day; and some tough competition leading to casualties among the weaker brethren thereafter.

As the scope of the change dawned on the City, what followed was like the first day of a Harrods sale. Respected firms in the City were snapped up, often for many times their paper value, in an orgy of purchases as rival groupings jostled with each other to buy market skills and position and build up financial conglomerates. The lesser-known names went too, if at somewhat less exalted prices. By the time the dust had settled an estimated £2 billion had changed hands, spent on buying and re-equipping existing firms, or on staffing and backing new ones. Many senior partners of stockbroking and jobbing firms retired to their newly acquired country estates to count the money. In the process a whole new jargon emerged: 'golden handshakes', 'golden hellos' – and 'golden handcuffs' – and the 'marzipan layer'. This last group consisted of those below the level of director or partner upon whom firms actually depend for their operations. They were worried that they might be left out as the bandwagon gathered pace, but in time, as it was realized how valuable they were, the riches percolated downwards to them. Those with expertise in, say, the analysis of electronic stocks, or knowledge of Far East bond dealing, found themselves snapped up at handsome salaries as the highly priced infantry of the Big Bang war.

In effect what was being created was a series of large securities houses: some British-owned, some owned from overseas. The most ambitious, such as Barclays Bank, have spent almost 10 per cent of their capital on buying their way into the market. Barclays bought two major Stock Exchange firms: the stockbrokers de Zoete and Bevan, and the jobbers Wedd Durlacher Mordaunt. To run the new operation, Barclays poached the respected vice chairman of Kleinwort Benson, Sir Martin Jacomb. At the time many in the City felt Barclays was gambling somewhat rashly. Many firms announced loudly that they would not be seeking amalgamation into large securities houses, but would instead concentrate on special-ist businesses: so-called 'niche' trading. Interestingly, City opinion now is that Barclays took the right course: in a recent poll of 100 City insiders, BZW (Barclays de Zoete Wedd, as the firm is now called), is rated as the firm most likely to succeed in the post-Big Bang City. Some way behind, but still ahead of the pack, was another British firm, Mercury International (formed around the merchant bank Warburgs). Two foreign rivals came next on the list: Merrill Lynch, the American securities house, and the Japanese giant Nomura. By contrast, 'niche' traders were overwhelmingly thought to have less chance of success. The interesting question now is how successful all these new conglomerates are actually going to be, and whether they are going to justify the fancy prices paid for their constituent elements. Already there are signs that it is proving to be a much more competitive marketplace – in December 1986 the *Economist* estimated that the abolition of fixed commissions had cost broking firms as much as one third of their income.

In all this turmoil the Bank's views and role were clear. As David Walker puts it, the Bank's aims were twofold: 'one objective is that London itself should become more significant globally ... a second objective, related but separate, is to have a significant role for British-owned players in that marketplace'. To ensure this, the Bank put a lot of effort into the marriage business, trying to put the right firms together into appropriately strong groupings. Rarely can the Bank's informal influence have been exercised more powerfully. As one insider puts it, somewhat disrespectfully, 'We went round ensuring that the jewels in the British Crown would not be left high and dry.'

Two areas in particular were of concern to the Bank: the gilts market and the policing of the new structure. Trading in gilt-edged stock (£262 billion in 1985) accounts for the bulk of the London

Stock Exchange's turnover: any change to the Exchange's rules was therefore of enormous interest to the Bank. In its gilts operations the Bank is basically concerned to fund the Government's deficit on an ongoing basis – and preferably at a price that keeps the cost of borrowing as low as possible.

In the pre-Big Bang days the gilts market was a cosy place with a small number of players: stock would be issued at a certain price and, by convention, it would be announced that it had all been taken up by the market at that price. (In practice this did not always happen and the Bank would be forced to buy unsold stock back onto the books of the Issue Department. From there it would be released onto the market as conditions allowed: so-called 'tap stock', because supply was turned on and off like a tap.) It was an easy system for the Bank to operate and worked well in its own quiet way. But it had its disadvantages: the number of players in the market was very small: by the time of Big Bang there were only half-a-dozen gilts jobbers, three of whom did the lion's share of the business. And it was expensive: even on a commission rate which was lower than that on the main Stock Exchange, the taxpayer was rewarding richly those firms which engaged in virtually risk-free business. The Bank's hope was that new entrants to the business – such as the large American market makers – would sell gilts actively through their marketing departments to their customers, thereby making the funding operation easier and cheaper.

In November 1984 the Bank laid out its view of how the new gilts market would work, and in April 1985, after consultation with various parties in the City, produced a revised version. Applications to become gilt-edged market makers were invited; in effect firms were asked to do in the gilts area what was happening in the field of equities. Various obligations and conditions that market makers would have to meet were laid down, and it was confirmed that the Bank would only deal with members of the Stock Exchange. The essence of the Bank's requirements was summed up thus: 'The basic obligation of the market makers will be to make, on demand and in any trading conditions, continuous and effective two-way prices at which they stand committed to deal, in appropriate size as discussed in advance with the Bank, thereby providing continuous liquidity for the investing public.' Any market maker who failed to fulfil these conditions was threatened with withdrawal of the Bank's goodwill and facilities. The existing system of issuing stock by tender was to continue, although the Bank announced that it intended to offer a gilts auction – a similar technique to that used in America – in the near future.

To the surprise of many in the City, there was a stampede of applications to become gilts market makers. In June 1985 the Bank announced the names of twenty-nine firms who had been accepted onto the list. Outsiders expressed surprise that so many firms believed there was money to be made trading in the gilt-edged market. Soon some of the new would-be market makers came to the same conclusion: before the market had even started operation, in March, Bank of America, already troubled by large losses at its US parent, pulled out in order to concentrate on markets where it had an established presence. It was followed in July by one of the City's best-known names, Union Discount, which concluded that there were too many market makers backed by too much capital for the operation ever to be profitable. In Union Discount's case, a quarter of a million pounds had already been spent on dealing equipment before the decision to withdraw was taken.

It is widely assumed in the City that the gilts market is where the first blood on the floor of Big Bang will be seen. The twenty-seven remaining market makers still seem too many to some observers. The Bank's official line is that it is up to the market to determine how many market makers it will support. It is already known in the City that one American firm suffered large losses in gilts trading in the run-up to Big Bang: sums of up to £20 million have been quoted. The less gloomy think that the internationalization of gilts dealing will result in a much more active market, as it has in America. In the United States there is a queue to join the Federal Reserve Bank's list of authorized primary dealers, and turnover in the market has increased sharply. Optimists note that in America a typical treasury issue changes hands every ten days, compared to every sixteen weeks in London. Were this pattern to be repeated in the City, there might be room for more market makers than pessimists fear. Whatever else happens, the new gilts market looks good news for the Bank and the taxpayer: the Bank has managed to produce a system in which it still has a powerful control over the workings of the market, while at the same time the sheer number

146

of players in competition for stock, which only the Bank can provide, makes it that much easier to sell gilts onto what can at times be a reluctant market.

On regulation, too, the Bank can claim a victory, albeit one that is already in question. In all the upheaval of the City's trading lifestyle, few thought to ask the views of the customers, in particular the big investing institutions, who are the main source of funds for the various markets. Many were worried at the end of single capacity, fearing that there would be a conflict of interest between the dealing and market-making sides of securities firms. Put simply, one part of the firm could be managing a new share issue, or holding a lot of stock in a company, and instruct its sales and marketing people to sell it to clients. The client would not know if the advice he was receiving from a dealer was unbiased or if he was getting the right price for what he was buying. One insurance company, the Clerical Medical and General, wrote to the Bank of England to voice these fears. The Bank hastened to reassure investors that the City would find a way of dealing with conflict of interest.

The debate had been started some years before, in 1982, with the publication of the Gower Report on investor protection. Professor Gower, a distinguished academic adviser to the Government, had been invited to review the procedures for protecting investors. He concluded, rightly, that the system was a mess and needed codifying so that anyone working in the field would be under a framework of clear comprehensive statute law, administered by a government agency. The City was horrified that its traditional system of self-regulation might be replaced by a statutory framework. As usual the Bank stepped into the breach. In what was widely seen as a pre-emptive strike in May 1984, the Governor of the Bank of England invited ten wise men from the City to join him in an informal committee to advise on the future of the City's self-regulatory bodies. In short order this committee concluded, to no one's surprise, that things were best handled if the City continued to regulate itself, though under overall statutory guidelines provided by Whitehall. In effect government was asked to delegate the job of policing the City to the City. It is not difficult to guess what the reaction would have been had the TUC suggested a similar scheme at the time when discontent over unbridled union power was running at its

147

height. But then the TUC did not have the Bank of England arguing its corner for it.

The Bank undertook to sell the solution to government. This it did successfully, and in a 1984 White Paper the Government accepted the Bank's view. Under the terms of the Financial Services Act, responsibility for regulating the City rests, in the first instance, with the Securities and Investment Board. Under the Board, and responsible to it, will come various self-regulatory agencies in the City. The extent of the Bank's victory was driven home by one clause in the Act, by which the Bank has effective control over the membership of the Board. This outraged many in Parliament – one, the Tory MP Anthony Beaumont-Dark, described this as 'a constitutional outrage. It gives the Bank the power to overrule the House.'

The sheer pressure of the run-up to Big Bang had worried many thoughtful souls, who wondered if the City could survive the shock to the system of so many changes happening at once. Yet, as the dust settles after Big Bang, those who helped it happen have much to be happy about. In particular the Bank, which played a key role in launching the City into the brave new world of international competition, congratulates itself on having made an omelette with remarkably few eggs going on the floor – so far. It must be emphasized again that the Bank did not have a battle plan drawn up in its head, or indeed any very clear long-term notion of where the revolution was going. All it did know was, as Montagu Norman had put it half a century before, that the caravan was moving on, and, if the City didn't want to be left behind, it had to move in step with the rest of the world. As Robin Leigh-Pemberton put it in his speech at the Mansion House dinner in October 1986, the changes that have happened 'have succeeded in releasing a great burst of energy and talent, not only in the Stock Exchange but in many other financial markets, and all of this is very healthy and very welcome. But we need to keep in mind that competition brings risk as well as benefits and can be a destructive as well as a constructive force.' The Governor went on to warn against the dangers of excessive competitive activity, while noting that losses and failures were part of the price of a free market. His final message was one of hope, even if it was delivered with much crossing of fingers and touching of wood: 'Let us hope, my Lord Mayor, when we come

28. *Malcolm Gill, head of Foreign Exchange Division, on the 'phone to the Treasury, keeping it informed of what's happening in the markets.*

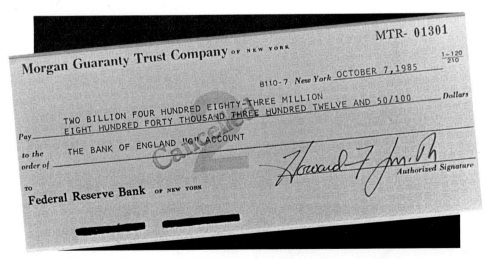

29. *A boost to the reserves: this cheque was the proceeds of a floating-rate note issue in the United States designed to boost the foreign-exchange reserves.*

30. *Top right: the formal dress of the Bank's doorkeepers – worn on Court days and ceremonial occasions – dates back to 1697.*

31. *Top left: John Head, furniture storekeeper, minds the dozens of clocks at the Bank.*

32. *Left: Gavin Laird, General Secretary of the Amalgamated Union of Engineering Workers, and a director of the Bank of England.*

to reflect upon the changes that have reached fruition during your mayoralty, we may see in them the beginning of yet another new and historic chapter in the City's story.'

9

The Brave New World and the Bank

The Bank of England is a very unusual and private place. It is hidden from prying eyes by a high curtain wall with no windows in it. If you try to gain access to the main building of the Bank through the magnificent front hall on Threadneedle Street there is a careful system of checks to find out if you are a welcome visitor. First the polite Mr Pointer, the Bank's senior gatekeeper, resplendent in his pink livery and top hat, will politely inquire of your business. If you are a regular visitor he will recognize you: Mr Pointer's proud claim is that he knows by name and face some 2000–3000 people. The Banking and Securities Departments are situated on either side of the entrance, and if your business lies with either of them you will be directed to the appropriate counter. The strangest people have business with the Bank of England. There was, for example, the lady who had put several hundred pounds into her washing machine with some clothes: Mr Pointer recalls that she arrived armed with the inside drum of the machine, which was pasted with bits of notes. The Issue Department sorted her problem out for her, and replaced some at least of the money she had lost. Others are not so fortunate: such as the two Spanish ladies who turned up at the Bank clutching some old white £5 notes. They turned out to be German forgeries from the last war, and the ladies' only reward was a pink slip acknowledging receipt of £300 worth of forged notes. Tourists and the inquisitive are told, with polite regret, that they cannot see the gold vault or the machines that print notes.

150

If, however, your business is with an official inside the Bank proper, you will be handed on to a receptionist and then to the Bank's security guards, who will only let you pass into the inner sanctum of the Bank if you are accompanied by a member of staff. The Bank's plain-clothes security guards do not have Mr Pointer's memory for faces or his trusting nature: passes must be shown by everyone – including the Governor. The degree of security they impose is intense to the point of being obsessional: it is as if the security force (recruited from former Special Branch and military police officers) sees itself as being charged with the reality behind the phrase 'safe as the Bank of England'.

Their greatest fear, an understandable if rather improbable one, is that someone will try to rob the Bank. It certainly wouldn't be an easy thing to do: the building is tremendously well built, with immensely thick walls and heavy doors. Security is tight and highly discreet. Nor, it has to be said, would there be much point in breaking in. There is surprisingly little of easily negotiable value in the Bank.

There is the gold of course – 'transient, shining trouble', as James Granger described it in the eighteenth century. The Bank has plenty of that, though it owns none of it. The many hundreds of millions of pounds' worth of gold held in the vaults of the Bank belong to the nation or the Bank's customers. Stealing any of it would be a feat. The vaults are far below ground, massively constructed of concrete and stainless steel, with complex hidden security systems in operation. And the vaults aren't anything like as romantic as Fort Knox. Contrary to one's expectations, they are a rather dull and unimpressive place despite the amount of wealth they contain. For the Bank, gold is just a commodity to be stored, a part of its commercial activity. The actual vaults are very plain rooms, drearily lit by strips of neon, and the gold bars are stacked on pallets in heaps only two or three feet high. (This is for the simple reason that if it was stacked any higher it would go through the floor.) The people who work in this rather dingy corner of the Bank do not treat gold with enormous respect: they look on it as if it was lead or any other cumbersome commodity. When a shipment of bars arrives, each is stamped with the Bank's own number, for reference, and weighed on a wonderfully old-fashioned, but, so one is assured, highly accurate machine.

Even if one did manage to break through to the vaults, an extraordinary amount of effort would be required to make a dent in the stocks of gold held there: gold bars are remarkably heavy things, much more cumbersome than one would think. (A standard bar is about the size of a building brick, and weighs 27 pounds: each is worth about £120,000.) The men working in the bullion area are therefore all fairly beefy. These guardians of the nation's assets preserve an especial contempt for the makers of the 1969 film *The Italian Job*, in which villains loaded up three Minis with gold and engaged in a breathtaking chase through the streets of Milan, pursued by the police. As one put it to me, 'with the amount of bars they put in those cars, they'd be standing on end, not driving'.

There is a fascinating nineteenth-century story of the directors of the Bank receiving an anonymous letter that requested that they meet the writer in the gold vault at midnight in order to learn something to their advantage: so the story goes, they eventually agreed to, and found a London sewerman inside the vault. He had gained entry to the gold vaults via the network of sewers beneath the Bank and wished to tell them of weaknesses in their security. Needless to say, official sources and records cast doubt on this romantic, if improbable, legend.

Gold apart, you could not steal much else of value from the Bank: as one official put it, 'You'd do better robbing your local Post Office.' The Bank still deals in real cash through its retail banking side, a legacy of its history. It maintains accounts for numerous departments of government, and for 150 or so banks and other financial institutions. In addition it holds accounts for a number of foreign central banks. It also holds personal bank accounts, but it is hardly in competition with the great clearing banks. It decided to retain its personal banking side in the 1960s, so as to keep experience of this aspect of the business going inside the Bank. The Chief Cashier, David Somerset, says that the Bank is willing to take on accounts 'in a very non-aggressive way'. As a recent article in the Bank's house journal, *The Old Lady*, put it, to have an account, one must be an individual 'of established standing in the local community'. Don't rush to transfer your money to Threadneedle Street; unless you have a very close relationship by way of business with the Bank, you will be politely turned away. Most of its ordinary account holders are Bank staff. The normal banking services are offered, although the limitations of the Bank's branch network are a problem. The cheque books are beautiful: elegant creations from an earlier age. (The cashpoint cards, by contrast, are just as ugly as every other bank's.) There is, though, one major disadvantage to banking at the Bank: overdrafts are strictly forbidden, and woe betide any Bank staff member who tries to bounce a cheque. It is as if the Bank is determined that its staff, at least, shall not be tempted to live beyond their means like the rest of the nation.

The most valuable asset stored at the Bank is information: a surprisingly large amount of it about the status and position of private companies, especially banks; and a lot of market sensitive information. Working at the Bank should be a golden opening for anyone interested in today's fashionable crime of insider dealing: yet, surprisingly enough, no Bank staff appear to succumb to the temptation. The apparent level of probity of those working at the Bank can't be due to how much they are paid – rates of pay are far below the level many of the staff could command in the commercial world. The Bank's hold on the loyalties of its staff is a mixture of the potent fix of power, and the feeling of being at the centre of events, tinged with a very British sense of duty.

With some justification the Bank likes to think it draws in a rather special sort of person: 'It's no good them coming in if they want to make money fast', says Deputy Governor George Blunden, 'or if they want to wield power quickly when they're young. They've got to be people who have high standards of integrity, a high sense of public duty and a great ability to work in a team.' Mr Blunden adds that it is important for any potential recruit to 'get the sense of the ethos of the place'. It has, he thinks, 'a sort of magic'.

The building itself is certainly a City landmark, though whether it is one that has much magic to it is another matter. In 1925 most of the old building, the creation of Sir John Soane, was demolished. In the decade and a half that followed a magisterial edifice seven storeys high, designed by Sir Herbert Baker, grew behind the curtain wall (almost the only part of Soane's original building to survive). It is an impressive building; but few would call it beautiful. Sir Nikolaus Pevsner went so far as to describe the demolition of Soane's Bank as, 'in spite of the Second World War, the worst individual loss suffered by London architecture in the first half of the twentieth century'. He complained bitterly that 'the use of Soane's masterwork as the footstool of a Herbert Baker seems unforgivable'.

No expense was spared in Baker's creation. The finest materials were used at every stage, and Baker clearly set out to create a building that would inspire awe. Everything is on a vast and formal scale – banker's rococo at its most unrestrained. The sheer solidity of its construction is now wreaking a terrible vengeance on today's occupants. For the past few years Bank staff have lived with the incessant noise of drills and jack hammers as labourers drive holes in Baker's massive walls to install the services essential to the electronic age – cable ducts and air-conditioning conduits and the like. The noise has become an accepted feature of life to those who work at the Bank, and insiders tend not to hear the din.

Despite the noise of the building work, inside is a very different world from the bustling streets of the City outside: at the heart of the Bank there is an inner sanctum of quiet – the Garden Court, one third of an acre of trees, grass and statuary. As the Governor jokes, given City land prices, it is probably the most expensive lawn in the world. Around it are the offices of the Bank's senior executives. It is perhaps symbolic that, whereas in most office buildings, the positions of power are those commanding views out into the world (corner suites at the tops of tower blocks are favourites in the City), at the Bank, the more powerful you are, the more your office looks inward.

The working atmosphere inside is also far removed from the hectic pace in the commercial world around. The Bank has the air of a large academic institution engaged on scholarly, but not very hurried, research projects. The dealers in the gilts room and in foreign exchange do take their jackets off, and work in shirtsleeves, like their counterparts elsewhere in the City; but the rest of the Bank manages to give the appearance of taking life at a more gentlemanly pace – as if to do otherwise might betray a lack of confidence that all is well. This is not to say, of course, that Bank officials do not work hard – certainly hours of work for some staff are very long indeed; it is just that they manage to give the impression of taking things slowly.

It is, of course, not quite like it used to be in Victorian times, when banking really was a leisurely occupation: in Jerome K. Jerome's novel *Three Men in a Boat*, it is said of one of the trio, George, that he 'goes to sleep at a bank from ten till four each day, except Saturdays, when they wake him up and put him outside at two'. Walter Bagehot, in his study of the late Victorian banker, noted that it was not a full time occupation; 'a certain part of his time, and a considerable part of his thoughts, he can readily devote to other pursuits'. At the Bank too, there was time for other pursuits; Kenneth Grahame, who rose to be Secretary of the Bank, was able to write *The Wind in the Willows* and other books while at the Bank.

The lifestyle was a relaxed one. At the end of the eighteenth century, a working year that was theoretically rather long (it included Saturdays) was in reality much shortened by the forty-seven bank holidays that then existed. Among those days celebrated was, suitably enough, the birth of William III. And hours of work were not exactly onerous: from 9 a.m. to 3.30 p.m. was standard at the beginning of the nineteenth century. Many clerks were allowed to run their own businesses on the side. (One Superintendent of the Drawing Office ran a wine business as his sideline.) The nineteenth century saw much tightening of this easy-going lifestyle. In 1836 the Court of Directors decreed that bankruptcy of staff members would lead to dismissal, as might frequenting public houses, smoking and singing. In the 1850s, when the fashion for moustaches became all the rage, the Bank authorities tried, with little success, to ban facial growth as being inconsistent with the dignity of the Bank: the official order stated that the authorities 'strongly disapprove of the practice, and if this hint be not attended to, measures will be resorted to which may prove of a painful nature'.

In reality though it seems that these strictures on staff behaviour were not necessary – Bank staff tended, then as now, to be somewhat sober in their lifestyles. Many were very hard-working too; it is recorded that Thomas Rippon, who worked at the Bank for fifty-three years, ending up as Chief Cashier at the age of seventy, took only one holiday during his years of service – and that he cut short after three days because he got bored.

On the whole the Bank has always been a good, if somewhat paternalistic, employer. In 1799 the Court ruled that certain vacancies for Bank jobs were to be open only to the sons of Bank employees with at least fifteen years service. Long dynasties were common – one family remained in the Bank's employ for 140 years. Three, four or five generations of service were, until recently, not uncommon. But not all Bank employees served so conscientiously; in 1803 one Robert Aslett, who had had a long and distinguished career and was then Second Cashier at the Bank, was tried for fraud. Aslett had purloined hundreds of thousands of pounds' worth of Exchequer bills that had already been cashed at the Bank and used them to back stock purchases. The ease with which he had managed to extract the bills led to a security system involving the use of dual keys that remains to this day.

The Bank was not ungenerous to its staff; paid holidays were introduced in 1845 (ranging from six to eighteen days depending on length of service). And various fringe benefits were introduced way in advance of the rest of the nation; a widows' fund was set up in 1791, a Provident Society in 1854, and a pension fund in 1870. But by the end of the First World War the staff was sufficiently unhappy with conditions of service to complain in a memorandum 'respectfully addressed to the Governor and Directors'. This memorandum noted that all over Britain workers were forming themselves into trades unions; 'it were a pity if trades unionism in any shape or form should enter within the walls of the Bank of England if it can be obviated now'. The staff went on to suggest various reforms in terms and conditions of service and the formation of a committee to represent the views of Bank staff. In conclusion the staff affirmed 'their loyalty and appreciation of the many benefits they enjoy in the service of the Bank, for whose dignity as the leading Bank in the country they are naturally jealous'. To this day most of the Bank's staff are represented by the Bank of England Staff Organization, rather than by any of the banking unions. The only stronghold of conventional trades unionism is at the printing works.

In the old days, the Bank could be a stern employer. Bert Marshall, who retired recently as Furniture Manager after almost forty-four years' service, recalls a martinet of a Principal in one of the clerical offices in his early days: 'he'd come round and tap you on the back and say "Marshall, seat under", and you'd get off your high stool, stick it underneath the desk and you would work standing for two hours. And then he'd let you sit down and another group would have to stand.' Marshall met his wife-to-be at the Bank, and that caused problems: 'Romance in the Bank was very much frowned on.' She was moved to another department, but got into trouble for using the wrong mirror in the ladies': 'they had mirrors for girls over twenty-one and mirrors for girls under twenty-one, and my wife was marched off to the powers that be because she was actually seen combing her hair in an over twenty-one mirror when she was only eighteen. She was told in no uncertain terms that this was not on.' The Bank tends to be firm with staff who don't live up to the high expectations it has of them: one young lady employee who appeared naked in a girlie magazine in the early seventies (thereby being promptly nicknamed by Fleet Street 'the naughty young lady of Threadneedle Street') was dismissed.

The nature of the staff employed by the Bank has changed much over time. The most important development of recent years has been the conscious cultivation at the Bank of professional central banking skills. By the end of the nineteenth century, the old structure – of 'visiting amateurs' (the part-time directors) assisted by 'working clerks' (the full-time staff of the Bank) – was proving unworkable. Under that system, the Governor and his deputy served two-year terms, during which they left their businesses in other hands and worked virtually full time at the Bank. The other directors, including the members of the various executive committees of the Bank, were part-time. The senior officials of the Bank, such as the Chief Cashier and the Chief Accountant, were full-time members of staff; but it was rare for them to share in the decision-making process. It was only in 1925 that, for the first time, a member of the Bank's staff, a former Chief Cashier, became a member of the Court.

During the long governorship of Montagu Norman, the level of professionalism of the Bank's key staff improved enormously. The complex international financial issues of those years necessitated a much higher quality of staff than had been required in the calm Victorian years. Many of those who trained under Norman went on to start Commonwealth and European central banks on the same principles as the Bank of England.

To the outsider the biggest surprise about the Bank of England is that most of the people working there are not in any sense central bankers. In fact, of the Bank's 5000 staff, only about 10 per cent are engaged in what can really be called central banking activities. Some 20 per cent of Bank staff work in the printing section; while almost 40 per cent are engaged in essentially clerical duties in the Banking and Registry Departments, and in corporate services. It would probably be true to say that the Bank employs more artisans than it does bankers; it has almost 700 craftsmen with a bewildering display of skills – fitters, welders, carpenters, joiners, plumbers, electricians, sheet-metal workers, upholsterers and french polishers to name a few – to maintain the Bank's fabric. This includes some 6000 pieces of antique or period furniture. In addition the Bank has its own water supply, drawn from an artesian well beneath the Bank (a warning, it produces quite ghastly coffee); and its own power station, capable of running the Bank if the London Electricity Board supply fails.

By contrast, the Policy and Markets Division of the Bank employs 340 people, the Finance and Industry Division just forty and the Banking Supervision Division 120. In common with many other institutions the Bank has recruited graduate trainees for many years. In the year ending February 1985, forty-eight graduate trainees were taken on, a substantial increase in numbers on the year before, and probably a reflection of a greater workload and the significant increase in the number of staff resignations. The Bank now encourages secondments of staff, its own to other institutions, and outsiders into the Bank, to widen experience.

If the picture that emerges is of an institution that seems remarkably untouched by the modern world, pursuing its own course untroubled by developments elsewhere, that would not be accurate. But there is a grain of truth in it. To go into the Bank is to pass into another world of old-fashioned and rather cautious values that has vanished elsewhere in the City of London. Just a few yards from the grand bronze doors of the Bank lies a completely different world, one that the Bank is simultaneously part of, and yet sets itself apart from. One curious Bank ritual illustrates the point.

Every morning, just before 9 a.m., a Bank official settles down to fill in a large piece of white paper, marked 'Secret' at the top. This paper is the 'Exchequer White' and is, in broad summary, the Bank's best estimate of the daily monetary needs of the banking system. Put simply, the Exchequer White indicates the flow of money; it has two parts to it – payments in and out of the banks, and those in and out of the Government's accounts. Thus at a very basic level, the individual paying £100 in tax represents a 'loss' of £100 to the liquidity of the banks and an addition of the same amount to the liquidity of the Government. At the same time the Government may be reversing that flow by paying out, let us say, a tax rebate of £200. Millions of such transactions are entered, in summary, on the Exchequer White. At the end of all those figures is a final calculation that indicates whether the system as a whole is going to be long or short of money for the day. At 9.45 a.m. the Bank issues a statement via Reuters indicating the final arithmetic and announcing whether it will be buying paper (that is to say, injecting money into the system if it is short) or selling it (that is, taking cash out if there is too much money around). The exercise is a fascinating one – and an essential, if mundane, part of the daily workings of the banking system.

But the way in which it is done is miles removed from the high-tech world of modern banking. Whereas most other institutions would have computerized the job, the Bank's official does it with the very simple technology of a pencil and an india rubber. The reason is an interesting insight into the Bank and the way it works: 'If it were done by computer', says Ian Thompson, who draws up the Exchequer White, 'the figures might be taken more as gospel; doing it by hand you are able to avoid those dangers. You can take reasoned judgements and take a view: it's very difficult to computerize something which contains elements of judgement.' It seems all rather quaint and old-fashioned at first sight; but, like much that the Bank does, there is method in the madness – a method that will probably last, and work, long after the last computer screen in the City has broken down.

To many in the City, the Bank seems a curious, very British type of institution, left over from earlier times: they wonder whether it can survive the pressures of the modern age. It is a question that has been asked about central bankers elsewhere in the world too. Observers wonder if these pillars of old-fashioned rectitude have a role any more. As markets grow in sheer size and become increasingly globalized in scope, the traditional controls exercised by central bankers are becoming ineffective. Some go so far as to say that central bankers as such are a dying species, doomed to watch and warn on the sidelines as the unrestrained enthusiasms of the markets cause the world economy to stumble into disaster.

It is certainly true that, over the last few years, central bankers have lost some of the power they once had to manage the system in the old ways. Developments in foreign-exchange markets illustrate the point well. As has been noted, the size of the worldwide foreign-exchange market is now so enormous that any central bank's ability to influence it is very limited: the emphasis now placed on technical adjustments and 'smoothing' processes is as much an admission of defeat as anything else. To achieve anything, central banks must act in co-ordination with each other. Since the collapse of fixed parties in the early seventies, it has been difficult to do this. But it happened in autumn 1985 when finance ministers and central bankers of the United States, Japan, France, Britain and Italy met in secret at the Plaza Hotel in New York. They agreed that the dollar was overvalued, and that co-ordinated action should be undertaken to bring it down. The announcement of the agreement was sufficient to start the slide; careful joint action thereafter reduced the value of the dollar worldwide. But no central bank could have done that on its own, nor can one country or government acting alone sustain a value for its currency that is not credible to the market.

At the same time changes in the rules of the foreign-exchange game have dramatically reduced the role of central bankers. The Bank of England was as astonished as most of the City when Mrs Thatcher's incoming Conservative Government abruptly abolished exchange controls in autumn 1979. At a stroke a chunk of the Bank's work, managing the controls, was rendered unnecessary. The Manchester branch, for example, lost half its staff. More important, a major change of thinking was forced on the Bank. A public relations film made for the Bank a few years ago, when exchange controls still existed, illustrates the point. It showed executives of the Bank in deep conversation with the Finance Director of ICI, one of Britain's biggest companies. ICI was seeking permission to buy dollars in order to build a factory in the United States. The film commentary noted that, once the Bank was convinced of the need for this, it would give ICI 'all possible help'.

Such a scene could no longer happen. Exchange controls are being removed all round the world: the free-market economic theories of today hold that it is entirely a commercial decision for ICI to decide where, when and with what it should build factories. The authorities have no role in the matter. The Labour Party has hinted that, if it wins the next election, exchange controls may be reintroduced, in some form, so as to prevent the outflow of capital.

But it is doubtful, given the worldwide and interlocked nature of financial markets today, whether such a policy could be carried out in practice. The very suggestion that controls were to return could well lead to a collapse of sterling, and scupper London's chances of ever again being a major player in the world's financial markets. Such realities have caused the Labour Party to back down, although it still threatens to penalize the holding of overseas assets. The lesson, yet again, is that no one country can afford to be out of step with other countries.

There has been much discussion as to what the role of a central bank should be in today's economic environment. Andy Mullineux, a lecturer in economics at Birmingham University, recently asked the question in a paper entitled 'Do We Need the Bank of England?' His answer was the somewhat Irish one that one did not, provided one did not start from here. If one was trying to create a central bank from scratch, one would land up with a very different animal from today's Bank. Mullineux suggested that most of its functions could be privatized at some saving to the state. Its function as note issuer could easily be performed, as in Hong Kong, by private banks. Again, as in Hong Kong, the management of foreign-exchange markets on behalf of government could be contracted out to a commercial bank.

Many other parts of the Bank's work could, he argued, be done elsewhere. The clearing banks could provide their own joint clearing and banking house. Even the traditional role of the Bank as lender of last resort could be handled by building up a compulsory insurance scheme to protect bank depositors as is used in several countries. (It is worth remembering that the 1979 Banking Act created just such a deposit insurance scheme to repay 75 per cent of money lost, up to £10,000, in a bank failure.) Banking regulation could be transferred, Mullineux suggested, to the Department of Trade and Industry (though some would wonder, remembering that Department's sorry experience with the Section 123 banks, whether this was a good idea). One of the Bank of England's oldest functions, running the National Debt, is nowadays essentially a large-scale computer operation which could just as well be carried out by a computer services company. The funding programme and operations in the gilts markets could be handled by a broker under contract to the Treasury. Mullineux concluded that the residual

161

functions surviving this wholesale privatization of the Bank of England could be carried out in-house at the Treasury.

This was precisely the weakest point in his theory. If the Bank's role in helping formulate monetary and economic policy were transferred to the Treasury, this would reduce the 'independent element' in policy-making. In the modern highly political world of economic management, government might welcome that: Mrs Thatcher is not the first, nor will she be the last, Prime Minister, to find any signs of dissent among her advisers unwelcome. The question is whether Parliament and the nation at large would welcome such a state of affairs. Even more to the point, the financial markets would be highly suspicious of economic and monetary policies that stank too strongly of politics because they emanated solely from the Treasury.

In addition Mullineux's analysis does not take into account the most important function undertaken by the Bank of England – the informal one of leadership in the financial community. This is the role which it is most difficult to define, depending as it does on the long-standing authority of the Bank, and the respect it has built up in financial circles. Mullineux's article was written before Big Bang, and thus did not take account of the key role played by the Bank in managing that dramatic change in the City's lifestyle.

But the Bank's very success in achieving this upheaval could also pose a threat. It is now left with finding a role for itself in the system post-Big Bang. Many have wondered if, by associating itself so closely with all these changes, and investing its authority so heavily in them, the Bank may not have opened itself up to the danger of having managed itself out of a job. The emphasis on free markets, operating with a much lesser degree of regulation, implies a much diminished role for the authorities – firms must be left to sink or swim on their own. But does that mean that whole markets will be allowed to go down in the name of non-intervention? Many feel that it will take one major financial crisis threatening the stability of the markets for there to be calls for a return to greater regulation. Not that it would be easy to legislate back into existence all the old powers of the central bankers: today's internationalized markets make it difficult for one country to act alone. Many think that the old days and the old ways are a thing of the past: former Labour Chancellor Denis Healey says that 'the tidy gentlemanly world in

162

which central bankers used to work in Britain has gone forever'.

The end of the days of gentlemanly behaviour places a question mark over the Bank's ability to exert its authority over some of the new players who will now be taking a role in London's markets. Many are huge by comparison with British firms and regard London as just another marketplace. For many of them it will not be their principal place of business. How will such institutions take to a quiet 'word in the ear' from the Bank of England? Many of them are large enough to ignore it and carry on as before, if not in London then elsewhere. The Bank and the Government has spent a lot of time and effort persuading new players to come and try their luck in London: what would be the point in then frightening them away? How anyway do you discipline firms in a world which has consciously thrown many of the old club rules out of the window?

The more optimistic hope that the new arrivals in the market will agree to be good boys. David Scholey, head of one of the largest British securities houses, Mercury, hopes that the Bank will not be forced to be more aggressive: 'If the practitioners, be they British or from other countries, take an attitude of increasing confrontation or take up the position of operating solely by the letter of the law, then it will be essential for the Bank to raise the profile to counter that. I don't think that will happen.'

So far the new players have been polite in the extreme about their hosts. Tom Strauss, Executive Vice President of the American giant Salomons, says diplomatically, 'As you participate in foreign markets you have to adapt to the tradition or standards and style of those marketplaces and to think that we should attempt to change the tradition here would be somewhat naïve. We look forward to learning more about the ways and traditions of the Bank of England.' Minoru Mori, London office manager for one of the largest Japanese securities houses, Daiwa, is equally charmed by the Bank: 'I think they are quite smart people and they are very experienced and knowledgeable.'

With the Japanese in particular, the Bank has been obliged to use a certain amount of discreet muscle. Britain opened up its financial markets to Japanese firms on the clear, and stated, understanding that Japan would reciprocate. So far the Japanese have not moved very speedily to open up their domestic financial markets to competition: in fact the process of deregulation in Japan seems to be going very slowly. The Bank has quietly threatened retaliation by hinting, as one insider puts it, that it could be 'a bit Japanese in return'. Licences and authorizations could get quite as lost amid the mass of official paperwork in Thread-needle Street as they seem to in the Japanese Finance Ministry.

At the back of the Bank's thinking is a complex balancing act that centres on regulation. Establish a regulatory framework that is too demanding, as happened in the sixties in New York, and you drive business away. American banks responded then by migrating to the freer environment of London, taking their extensive business with them. No one wants to repeat that mistake at a time when business can go anywhere there is a telephone line. At the same time none of the world's authorities wish to get involved in a Dutch auction, seeing who can throw the rules and regulations out of the window fastest. If each market tried to compete with its rivals in offering a free and easy system of trading, there would be little hope for effective investor protection.

That point was driven home with some force to the authorities in the Netherlands in 1986. A number of quite unregulated securities companies set up shop in Holland and started marketing stocks by telephone. All of them just happened to be in companies that were not yet listed on any exchange, but had, extraordinarily enough, just patented a revolutionary new product that was set to transform the world. In each case the company was – of course – about to be taken over by a well-known large company, with a resultant handsome capital profit for shareholders. Many investors fell for these sales pitches: in one such fiddle some 1200 British investors managed to lose £4.2 million. Now the Dutch authorities have cracked down and closed most of these bucket shops. They have had to move further afield to Spain or Cyprus, countries where the regulatory system is somewhat weaker.

The essence of the problem facing central bankers, as has been noted, is that you cannot nowadays confine any regulatory system to one country: the regulators must mimic the markets and become international. The problem of controlling banks was the first to be tackled on an international basis. This has been dealt with at numerous meetings of central bankers from round the world, most of which have taken place under the aegis of the Bank for International Settlements in Basle. This is the central bankers' club, set up in 1930 to act as a clearing house for co-operation between central banks. (They are a rather lonely breed, with none of their own to talk to at home: at the monthly Basle meetings, attended by every senior world central banker, problems can be discussed in confidence, and possible solutions aired.) The difficulty is that the regulators have had to run very quickly in the last ten years to catch up with the fast-moving financial marketplaces of the world. Devising new measures of control is a much slower process than inventing new financial instruments. The Bank has played a leading role in devising new supervisory and regulatory systems. For example, the Bank of England was the first to warn of the possible hazards of 'off-balance-sheet risks': that is, liabilities entered into by banks which, because of their nature, do not appear on a bank's balance sheet, despite being exceedingly risky. There are now signs that such hard work is paying off: at the beginning of 1987, the Bank of England and America's Federal Reserve Board announced an agreement on the minimum acceptable levels of bank capital that regulators in the two countries would require. In their announcement, they expressed the hope that Japanese regulators would join in this agreement.

The central problem with regulation, at home as well as abroad, is working out the relative positions of the regulators and the practitioners – deciding how far the first should be behind the second. In a free market, one adapting to change and customer demand, the regulator must clearly not be in front of the market, forbidding people to do things before they have even thought of doing them. That would negate the concept of markets and deny them their flexibility and capacity to innovate. At the same time, it is no use the regulator being miles behind the market, reacting to circumstances that prevailed months or years ago. The ideal position is, as one Bank official puts it, 'just a step behind the practitioners – close enough to see why and how something is happening, but not so close that you inhibit new ideas'.

Such a position is a subtle one: and not one you can easily legislate for. Because of its belief that only insiders fully understand how markets work, and therefore how to stay one step behind the practitioners, the Bank fervently supports a regulatory system that, while backed by legal powers, has a large degree of input in the form of marketplace experience. By contrast it believes that one

165

relying solely on statute, even when guided by carefully drafted rule books, would be hopelessly out of step most of the time, and incapable of flexible response to changing conditions in the market. Worse still, such a system would be at the mercy of the passing whims of ministers and MPs. The Bank has therefore invested a great deal of its authority in the view that Whitehall's watchdogs should stand back from frontline involvement in the City's marketplaces. (This does not, of course, apply in banking supervision, where the Bank acts under clear statutory provision provided by the Banking Acts. Even so in this area the Bank prefers to exercise its powers with, where possible, the consent of those it regulates.) The Bank's biggest worry is that those being regulated do not appreciate the benefits of having a say in their own regulation: in the 1985 annual report, Governor Robin Leigh-Pemberton said, somewhat plaintively, 'The City has a long tradition of regulation by consensus and the principle of being bound by the spirit of the rules as much as by their letter. I would like to see this tradition survive.' This thought was repeated time and again in the run-up to Big Bang. Some have found such appeals for gentlemanly behaviour hopelessly naïve: Denis Healey remarked disparagingly that it reminded him 'very much of the American Ambassador after the war in the Security Council who appealed to the Jews and Arabs to behave like Christians'.

A delicate system of regulation of the City has been lovingly created by the Bank and the Government, with the Securities and Investment Board at the top and a series of SROs – self-regulatory organizations – beneath it, covering separate areas. The Bank retains responsibility for overseeing the wholesale money and foreign-exchange markets of the City, while other markets are creating their own SROs. The system combines the ultimate backing of statute law with the ability for day-to-day regulatory practice to develop by experience and negotiation. Whether it will all work has yet to be seen, as it will only come into effect some time after Big Bang. As this book is being completed, arguments are still raging about the rules of the various self-regulatory bodies. Those outside argue that the SROs will be too weak; those inside threaten, as some of the securities companies have with the Eurobond market, to take their business elsewhere if certain proposed trading rules are enforced. The balance is clearly a difficult one to strike. Recent events have already cast a shadow over the whole system of self-regulation.

It seems one of the unwritten rules of financial scandals that, when they happen, they come, in rather Shakespearian fashion, in battalions rather than as single spies. The sudden fall of American financier Ivan Boesky, and the ensuing, almost daily, revelations of insider-trading scandals at first enthralled the City. Then, when a major public company, Guinness, saw its share price collapse and several of its leading executives forced from office in the wake of accusations of share rigging during the Distillers' takeover in 1986, the feeling turned to one of apprehension. As the investigation into the Guinness affair spread, and began involving some of the most blue-chip names in the City, including brokers and merchant banks, an atmosphere of near panic took hold.

Although City opinion was alarmed at all this, what was really worrying was the impact of these scandals on the perceptions of the public and the politicians. For the first time the exact workings of financial regulation became a major issue. Roy Hattersley, deputy leader of the Labour Party, and Shadow Chancellor, launched into a series of speeches with City regulation as their theme. Other Labour spokesmen openly attacked the Government for 'protecting' its friends in the City, and promised that, if elected, they would introduce a much stricter, state-managed system of regulation. Both the believers in the existing system of regulation and the advocates of more state intervention believe that the current spate of scandals has strengthened their case: one side has said that the very fact that someone has been caught proves that the system works; while the other side has claimed that the capture of just a few offenders proves that hundreds more are getting away with it.

It is not at all clear who is in the right in this particular argument. Certainly the old system, which relied entirely on self-policing, produced few results. Take insider trading as an example. Over the last few years literally hundreds of cases in which there were suspicious movements in share prices before significant announcements have been investigated by the Stock Exchange. Despite such movements being clear *prima facie* evidence of insider dealing, in none of them was the case proved, and no one was punished. In every case those profiting from such movements got away with it. However, on the other side of the argument, it is by no means clear that any full system of state regulation would end such activities: the United States, after all, has had the Securities and Exchange Commission for some years, but still produces just as many scandals.

The Government responded to claims of favouritism towards its friends in the City with distinct signs of panic. Urgent inquiries were ordered into specific cases, with ministers promising severe punishment for wrongdoers. Changes in the law were promised to increase the penalty for insider trading to a maximum of seven years. Both the Government and the Bank hope that the current regulatory regime can be made to work, and are worried that troubles in the City will undermine its credibility before it can get going. Fresh scandals will inevitably reflect badly on both the Government and the Bank. The Government will be seen to be associated with a state of affairs that lets its 'friends' in the City appear to get away with committing criminal actions, while the Bank will be viewed as, at best, tolerating this, and at worst conniving at creating the system that allows villains free rein in their operations.

The Bank has taken somewhat more pragmatic steps to ensure that order is restored to the City: steps that are a classic example of its informal powers in operation. The Bank's view was that swift and sharp action was what was required, not lengthy legal inquiries that might or might not lead to convictions. When asked by an anguished Department of Trade for advice on the tangled state of affairs at Guinness, the Bank's response was direct; in the words of one insider, 'we suggested that what was needed was to give the tree a bloody good shake'. Before Christmas 1986 one of its executive directors called in the independent directors of Guinness and asked them to consider the position of Ernest Saunders, the chief executive of the company. Shortly after the board dismissed Mr Saunders. When the scandals spread to Morgan Grenfell, Guinness's merchant bank advisers during the Distillers' takeover, again the Bank acted speedily and with little regard for social niceties. Morgan Grenfell's board were told in no uncertain terms that attempts to pin the blame for questionable operations in support of Guinness's share price on the over-enthusiasm of junior executives would not wash. Within days the chief executive and head of corporate finance at Morgan Grenfell had resigned. The same treatment was meted out to Lord Spens, head of corporate finance at Ansbachers merchant bank, who had helped Morgans in their operations. No one knows how much further the affair will spread – the Bank in particular stands to be embarrassed if the firm of Freshfields, Guinness's legal advisers during the battle, and also solicitors to the Bank, gets dragged into the scandal.

The Bank's hope is that a few immediate and well-publicized executions will serve *pour encourager les autres* and restore public confidence in the City. So far it seems to be working. Public anxiety about the City and its morals is markedly lower than it was at the end of 1986. But everyone is aware that, if the current bout of City scandals continues, further formal and statutory controls over the financial markets are a certainty. Indeed, at the end of January 1987, in a speech, the Governor of the Bank warned the City that failure to respect not just the law but also 'the accepted canons of best practice' in takeover battles would lead to the end of the present voluntary code and the imposition of one 'incorporating statutory powers of enforcement and statutory sanctions'. He made it clear that the City had more to lose from such a system than it would gain. In a reference to the Bank's actions in the Guinness affair he concluded that, in his view, the current mix of formal and informal powers was the right one: 'working within a statutory system our influence can be decisive and firm'.

The current crisis in the City has shown the Bank at its most effective, operating in its traditional ways, and pulling other people's chestnuts out of the fire. Throughout its long history it has worked like that; using informal authority and prestige – and methods – on countless occasions to make things happen that otherwise would not have happened (and could not have been persuaded to happen by the best endeavours of politicians and civil servants); or to stop things happening that otherwise would have. It has rarely acted with any firm philosophical basis for its operations, and sometimes even without a desired outcome in mind; it prefers to work prag-matically, feeling its way towards workable solutions and new situations. More than most, the Bank knows that crystal-ball gazing is a hazardous occupation: its experience in the past is that all too often no one was able to foresee what might or might not happen and therefore legislate for or against it.

The same is true of Big Bang: commentators speculate endlessly on where it is leading the City, and try to define a course for the future. The real fascination of Big Bang is precisely that it is a leap in the dark. No one knows what the eventual outcome of it will be; London may regain its leading position in the financial world, or the whole exercise of worldwide deregulation may end, as some fear, in a 1929-style market collapse on a global scale. Nor can the Bank of England guess where it will stand at the end of the process; but, if history is anything to go by, the Bank is likely to ensure that it stays somewhere near the heart of things, managing affairs quietly behind the scenes, and discreetly tidying up the mess left by yet another mountain of disappointed hopes. It would be strange if history did not repeat itself with the inevitable cycle of grand expectations fuelling a boom, followed by a crash. (Already observers are looking out for the first casualties of Big Bang.) If that is the case, the Bank of England will know what to do – it has, after all, been there several times before in its long history. Nor would a crash surprise the Bank – as has been noted, central bankers generally have a poor view of human nature. Like Alexander Pope at the time of the South Sea Bubble, the Bank of England may feel that Big Bang was just another of the follies and misfortunes of greedy men:

At length corruption, like a general flood
Did deluge all, and avarice creeping on
Spread like a low born mist and hid the sun.
Statesmen and patriots plied alike the stocks,
Peeress and butler shared alike the box,
And judges jobbed and bishops bit the town,
And mighty dukes packed cards for half a crown –
Britain was sunk in lucre's sordid charms.

Further Reading

Acres, W. Marston, *The Bank of England from Within* (Oxford University Press, 1931).

Andreades, A., *History of the Bank of England 1640–1903* (Frank Cass, 1966).

Bagehot, Walter, *Lombard Street: A Description of the Money Market* (first published 1873; numerous editions since).

Bank for International Settlements, *50th Anniversary Publication* (BIS, Basle, 1980).

Bank of England, Annual Reports.

——, *Bulletin* (published quarterly by the Bank).

——, *The Future Structure of the Gilt Edged Markets* (Bank of England, April 1985).

Barnet, Joel, *Inside the Treasury* (André Deutsch, 1982).

Boyle, Andrew, *Montagu Norman* (Cassell, 1967).

Bruce-Gardyne, Jock, *Ministers and Mandarins* (Sidgwick and Jackson, 1986).

Chapman, Stanley, *The Rise of Merchant Banking* (Allen and Unwin, 1984).

Clapham, Sir John, *The Bank of England 1694–1797*, 2 vols (Cambridge University Press, 1944).

Clay, Sir Henry, *Lord Norman* (Macmillan, 1957).

Coppieters, Emmanuel, *English Bank Note Circulation 1694–1954* (Louvain Institute of Economic and Social Research, 1955).

Donaldson, Peter, *Guide to the British Economy* (Pelican, 1965).

Galbraith, John, *Money* (André Deutsch, 1975).

Giuseppi, John, *The Bank of England: A History from its Foundation in 1694* (Evans, 1966).

Hamilton, Adrian, *The Financial Revolution* (Viking, 1986).

Longford, Elizabeth, *Wellington, Pillar of State* (Weidenfeld and Nicolson, 1972).

Mackenzie, A. D., *The Bank of England Note: A History of its Printing* (Cambridge University Press, 1953).

McRae, Hamish and Cairncross, Francis, *Capital City* (Methuen, 1985).

Moran, Michael, *The Politics of Banking* (Macmillan, 1984).

Pen, Jan, *Modern Economics* (Pelican, 1965).

Plender, John and Wallace, Paul, *The Square Mile* (Century, 1985).

Revel, John, *The British Financial System* (Macmillan, 1973).

Rosenberg, Kate and Thurston Hopkins, R., *The Romance of the Bank of England* (Butterworth, 1933).

Sampson, Anthony, *The Moneylenders* (Hodder and Stoughton, 1981).

Sayers, R. S., *The Bank of England 1891–1944*, 3 vols (Cambridge University Press, 1976).

Smith, Adam, *Paper Money* (Macdonald, 1982).

Select Committee on Nationalized Industries, *Report on the Bank of England*, 1975–6 session (Her Majesty's Stationery Office, 1976).

Index

173